It's A Miracle They Ain't Dead Yet

It's A Miracle They Ain't Dead Yet

✦

Welcome to the Texas Café

Kenneth Suna

iUniverse, Inc.
New York   Bloomington

It's a Miracle They Ain't Dead Yet
Welcome to the Texas Café

iUniverse books may be ordered through booksellers or by contacting:

iUniverse
1663 Liberty Drive
Bloomington, IN 47403
www.iuniverse.com
1-800-Authors (1-800-288-4677)

ISBN: 978-1-4401-6334-0 (pbk)
ISBN: 978-1-4401-6336-4 (cloth)
ISBN: 978-1-4401-6335-7 (ebk)

Printed in the United States of America

iUniverse rev. date: 11/02/09

This book is dedicated to my mom, Lila.
This is your book, too.

Contents

Author's Note

I was three years old when I saw Hulk Hogan body slam Andre the Giant. From the dramatic moment Hogan ripped his shirt in half, I knew I would be a professional wrestler.

I attended the best schools, public and private, in Washington, D.C. But I never intended to pursue a college education. While my high school friends discussed the colleges they would apply to, I spent my senior year investigating wrestling training schools. My mother warned me to have a back-up plan. But a single passion can limit your focus.

After graduating from the Edmund Burke School, I moved to Andover, Massachusetts, found a job, and rented a room in the home of a nice family. The move from a major city to a quaint town was jarring. I attended the Chaotic Training Center, from which several well-known wrestlers had graduated. Doubts about my chosen profession crept in following several brutal hours of being slammed into a wood- and steel-framed ring, thrown into telephone cables wrapped in duct tape (the ring ropes), and thrown over the top rope. I overshot the protective mat and smashed onto the cement floor. The pain that blasted down my legs and into my feet resulted in an appointment with an orthopedist.

"You've got a rather substantial crack in your vertebrae. Was there an inciting incident that caused this?"

My desire to move forward on my life-long dream had turned into a fear that was proving to be a large impediment. I spoke with Chad Wicks, a champion from the local wrestling territory later employed by the WWE. He told me not to force my dream now; doing so might lead to bigger disappointment. I packed my bags and moved home, heartbroken.

I had no Plan B.

I earned certification as a personal trainer, but the truth was, this was not a career I wanted to pursue.

What next? I found a job as an expediter in a popular neighborhood restaurant, the Texas Café. Later I would work in a high-end seafood restaurant, White Spice. I never intended to write a book. My mom moved to Manhattan and missed my nightly tales of restaurant horror. I e-mailed her these stories and began to compile them in a journal. Could I turn these stories into a book? Would it be a comedy? A thriller? A horror novel? I had seen so much in my three years in the restaurant business that all three genres seemed suitable.

During my time in the restaurant business, I interacted with characters from all walks of life and learned about human nature. I met folks who tested the boundaries of ethics. I worked for managers with questionable skills and lack of sound judgment despite their college degrees. I met El Salvadorians who became American citizens. They worked two or three jobs while sharing a one-room apartment with many coworkers. These hard-working immigrants sent more than half of their incomes home to help their wives and children.

I saw rats the size of cats, roaches that belonged in alien movies, and unsanitary acts, including a dishwasher who urinated in the kitchen drain. I saw cooks do lines of coke off the beds of their pick-up trucks prior to a busy dinner rush. I saw a cook drop a gallon of boiling water on his arm and watched his skin melt. My life was threatened by a crazed dishwasher.

My decision to postpone college might seem shortsighted to many parents. But there are many routes to success, and of course, success can be defined in so many ways. College students mature intellectually, but do they learn to apply their knowledge in practical situations? In a healthy economy, jobs in your chosen field are within reach for a college grad with connections. Promotions follow, assuming you can do the job for which you were trained. But consider yourself lucky if you're a college grad with no connections. You may have to settle for a lesser job than that for which your education prepared you, but you'll get a glimpse into a world you never expected to experience. You'll develop a deeper understanding of employees' motivations and work ethics.

This would-be wrestler learned about the working world and matured in the process. Everything you will read about the two restaurants I worked in is true. Some of the stories may stun you or gross you out. Many will make you laugh. I've experienced these reactions and more. The names of restaurants and individuals have been changed to protect not the innocent but the guilty.

I hope you'll develop greater empathy for hard workers at the bottom rung, whether it's the server you may think is your personal slave or the busboy you call over to clean up your mess. This comes at you not from a chef de cuisine, restaurateur, manager, or investor. This comes at you from a twenty-one-year-old employee. This is your eye-opening, jaw-dropping, gut-wrenching exposé that will have you saying,

"It's a miracle they ain't dead yet."

Chapter One
Texas Café 101

I walked down Wisconsin Avenue with the intent of going into every store and restaurant until I was hired. I thought I would need a month or two at most to figure out what I wanted to do with my life.

I went into a well-regarded neighborhood barbecue place. It wasn't hiring. I tried Blockbuster. No luck. I skipped the Texas Café. I'd eaten there once and swore I'd never go back. I went into an Italian-American pizza place. It wasn't hiring.

I was running out of options in my neighborhood. I set my sights on the Texas Café. I met Stephanie, who was bartending, and asked if the restaurant was hiring. She called Meghan, who came downstairs and introduced herself as the general manager.

"So, you want to be a waiter? Welcome aboard." Three minutes into our conversation, I was hired.

I began training with Stephanie, a skinny redhead who towered over me. She was well over six feet and smelled like stale cigarettes.

After my first week of training, I told Stephanie and Meghan that waiting tables wasn't my thing. I was about to tell them I would look for work elsewhere when Stephanie cut me off and asked if I would prefer working in the kitchen as an "expo." I accepted the job before I even knew what it was. Just like that, I became an expediter. I garnished dishes to enhance the meal's appeal, something the cooks and waiters neglected to do.

As an expediter, I relied on the help of the floor manager, Devon. Devon was a cocky, smooth-talking guy who wanted to try out for the Washington Redskins. This goal may have been the reason he was the definition of a team player. He helped anyone at anytime and wasn't

1

embarrassed to do tasks that other managers considered beneath them.

Devon asked me, "What do you eat with?"

"Uh, mouth?"

"Wrong, you eat with your eyes first. The food could taste like *shit,* but make the food look good and you're halfway there."

Seventy-nine out of eighty new restaurants fail every year. A lot of factors go into a restaurant's success. At the Texas Café, the quality of food was not one of them. Directly across the street was an authentic Mexican restaurant. Its food was purchased daily and was top quality. The same could not be said for the Texas Café. Food was delivered boxed and frozen.

So why was the Texas Café more popular? Both restaurants had similar pricing. The neighborhood was politically liberal and family oriented—the type of neighborhood you'd think would want to support the small, family-run place instead of the corporate restaurant. But that wasn't the case. The Texas Café had a bar for adults and also appealed to families with children. The walls were brightly colored and decorated with images of lizards, cowboys, and herds of cattle. Children were greeted with a pack of crayons and a place mat to draw on. Their artwork was displayed on the walls. The staff was friendly. In comparison, the authentic place lacked vitality. The Texas Café was constantly busy. The atmosphere was more appealing than the quality of the food.

Still, I had to make the food look good. After I put the finishing touches on the food, I placed the dish on a tray with the ticket from the line cook. A waiter took the food to the diner. Initially, that was it.

My sudden promotion was a challenge, though, especially when the restaurant was busy. The tricky part was remembering which garnish accompanied each dish. After White Spice, I realized I had it easy at the Texas Café. But this was my first job, and at the time, it was a lot to remember.

Chicken wings came with lettuce and a side of ranch dressing with a dollop of corn relish. Nachos came with guacamole and pico de gallo (pico for short). If they were veggie nachos, they got sour cream. Taquitos got a bowl of tomato chipotle and sour cream squiggles. Queso got a dollop of pico. Queso fun dito came with chorizo sausage, sour cream, guacamole, and pico.

Burritos and enchiladas always got shredded lettuce, sour cream, and guacamole. Tacos and quesadillas got lettuce, sour cream, and pico as a standard. Beef tacos were garnished with cheese and jalapeño peppers. Chicken tacos got cheese with corn relish on the side.

Shrimp and fish tacos got cabbage slaw and chipotle mayo squiggles. Crab and shrimp quesadillas got guacamole and corn relish. Tuna tacos got fajita onions and peppers and tomato chipotle sauce.

Fajitas, the most popular dish, got rice, beans, four flour tortillas, and a side plate of lettuce, cheese, guacamole, sour cream, and pico. But different proteins got different rice and beans. Seafood and vegetable fajitas got vegetarian-friendly black and green (black beans and white rice with green chile sauce) whereas beef, chicken, and carnitas (pork) all got red and red (red rice prepared with chicken stock, tomato puree, and onions and red beans with an ass-load of bacon).

You with me so far?

Any combination of meat and veggies got black and green in case the diners were kosher (unless the diners ordered carnitas and veggies). Combo platters got lettuce, sour cream, guacamole, and pico with the exception of the taco platter, which got everything but guacamole. Big platters—chicken, steak, and ribs—all got steak knives. Ribs got handiwipes.

Caesar salad came with paprika dots on the rim of the plate. (If you placed the dots correctly, they could be connected in the shape of the Texas Star.) Fajita salad was garnished with paprika and guacamole, and taco salad came with guacamole and sour cream. Tuna sandwiches were garnished with an avocado fan and chipotle mayo. All other sandwiches, with the exception of the plain chicken sandwich, got chipotle mayo. The plain chicken sandwich got lettuce and tomato.

However, I couldn't garnish a thing until the line cook gave me the ticket. What if I garnished a tuna sandwich before I got the ticket and the customer had specified no mayo? Oops. Eventually, the system changed so the line cook's printer included a carbon copy for me. This excellent addition to the routine eliminated the panicked need to garnish all the food in an order at once and allowed me to garnish entrees as they hit my window. I now assumed responsibility for coordinating all cooking times.

Tickets were hung in the window in the order they arrived: 6:30, 6:37, 6:42, and so on. An order that came through at 6:30 should theoretically come out first, but it rarely did. Certain foods took longer to prepare and cook. When the line cooks completed an order, they gave me their original copy. I matched it to my carbon copy and placed the food on a tray. Now the food was ready to be sold (or taken to the table). The cooks told me that when an order was ready, all I had to do was shout "runner" for someone to run the food.

I took to the job right away. I like to cook, so being in the kitchen was a perfect fit. When things slowed, I watched the food preparation and picked up cooking tips.

The kitchen staff made me feel welcome, and even better, I was learning more useful Spanish in the kitchen than I had ever learned in high school.

Deena, a beautiful brunette host, was Stephanie's cousin. She often visited the kitchen to snack on chips and queso. Sammy, a bartender, insisted Deena was a few fries short of a happy meal. Deena was a good sport, though, and we often had a good laugh over something ditsy she had done. She laughed along with us.

One evening a woman came in with a puppy in her purse and asked if she could have dinner. Deena, love-struck with the puppy, showed the woman to her seat. A health inspector could have shut us down.

A week later, Deena was snacking in the kitchen when Sammy came in and said, "Deena, there's a woman who wants a table."

Deena was on her way to the host stand when Sammy stopped her and said, "She wants to know if she can bring in her giraffe."

Three months into my employment, Deena casually mentioned that she was paid $8.50 an hour. I was shocked. I was only paid $6.50!

I went to Meghan and asked what was going on. She quickly realized her mistake. The training salary for a waiter was $6.50. She had forgotten to change my hourly rate to $8.50 when I made the switch to expo.

Pico de gallo sat in a plastic container on ice at the expo station. Since tomatoes release water constantly, the pico had to be drained from time to time. Tim, a waiter, reminded me to drain the tomatoes. His customers didn't like soggy tomatoes. He was kidding, but what did I know?

Still new, I had no idea how mischievous Tim was. He stormed into the kitchen one night with the most furious expression.

"Hey Ken! I got this from one of my customers!"

He threw a piece of paper at me.

"Dear Expo, the tomatoes were soggy and wet. You did not drain them. signed, Dissatisfied Customer."

I was shocked.

"Who wrote this?"

SMOOTH MOVE, BUTTER FINGERS, PART ONE

As my skills improved, I decided the time was right for self-promotion. The great thing about the Texas Café at that time was its management. Managers encouraged employees to express any ideas that might contribute to the restaurant's success.

My self-promotion included running food when I had the time. I had no idea that this was such a help to the waiters, who sometimes were in the weeds with their tables. Waiters were able to spend more time with their customers when I ran food.

My fear about carrying the tray was, of course, the dreaded tray drop. Karmah, a waiter, had been at the Texas Café for three years and had dropped only one tray.

I've seen some pretty good tray drops, but the best belonged to Alex, a manager. It was his *first* day at the Texas Café, and he was carrying a tray full of sizzling fajitas. He was heading toward the upstairs dining room and missed a step. Sizzling onions and sour cream? Everywhere.

Lucky for me, the dreaded tray drop eluded my Texas Café career. But would this disastrously embarrassing event rear its ugly head later on?

THE THREE AMIGOS

Three managers ran the Texas Café. Meghan was the general manager, Milton was the kitchen manager, and the floor manager was Devon. Milton was always creating fun dishes for the menu, like a chocolate banana burrito. Devon focused on customer satisfaction, and Meghan made sure everything ran smoothly. What a great intro to the restaurant business. I didn't realize how lucky I was.

These three managers never hesitated to help with anything anyone needed, especially when the restaurant was busy. They weren't demanding or nasty. When they asked for a favor, I was happy to help.

Before my coworkers and I knew it, Meghan was leaving to take on a more demanding restaurant in the Texas Café chain. Since our location was the smallest, it was used as a training ground for the chain's larger-volume restaurants. We were upset with Meghan's announcement. She deserved her promotion; we dreaded her departure. But Meghan assured us we would love her replacement, a woman named Joan.

People warned me about the real world. "It's a scary place." "You're going to be miserable." Well, they were wrong. My first few months on the job were awesome. I had great managers and got along with every coworker. Why are "real world" warnings so dire? So much for the harsh and ruthless world of liars and back-stabbers. In my mind, it didn't exist ... until Joan arrived.

Then I officially entered the real world.

Chapter Two

Fear Joan

Joan came right out of the 1954 Godzilla movie, except she wasn't a fifty-foot-tall lizard. The Texas Café resembled Tokyo, a once-innocent community now sent into a frenzy of fleeing, terrified people.

When Joan arrived, the staff agreed she seemed okay. Joan was a skinny, feisty, flirtatious blonde. Her bubbly personality resembled Meg Ryan's. She was inquisitive about how we performed our jobs, asking numerous questions. We were happy to fill her in.

But in a rather quick turn of events, we realized that Joan's friendly, calm exterior was an act. Underneath her "act nice because you're new" gimmick was the soul of a demon.

Before you could blink your eyes, she had turned the Texas Café into a by-the-book restaurant. This wasn't what the Texas Café was about. We were a fun place with a relaxed environment. Suddenly, we were run like a five-star, uptight business. The rules changed overnight. No more eating in the kitchen. If you wanted to eat, you came in early. Your ass was in trouble if you so much as nibbled on a tortilla chip.

We'd sneak a bite to eat when Joan wasn't around. We stood guard in the kitchen, looking through the window, while someone made a quick taco. We'd shout a warning when we saw her coming. Whoever was eating would shove the food into his face and run out the back door before she entered the kitchen.

If Joan caught you eating, she shouted, "Did you ring that in? Are you going to pay for that? We have to account for every item of food that goes out!"

She was loud, dramatic, overbearing, and volatile.

Prior to being the GM, Joan had owned two restaurants. Restaurant life means you anticipate and enjoy chaos. Joan hated the hectic nature of the business. The busier we became, the more ferocious she got. She yelled at waiters in front of customers and never understood that remaining calm was beneficial for the whole team. Yell at one employee and all employees are on guard.

Joan's inability to handle stress resulted in tantrums. In addition to being mean, Joan was often drunk. When the dining room was busy, she ran upstairs for a drink. The smell of alcohol on her breath became a fixture.

She also didn't want to spend so much as an extra dime.

During her first week, Joan hired Brad as a waiter. He looked young, but he insisted he had many years of experience. Brad showed himself to be a pro when it came to working a busy floor. We became fast friends when we discovered we shared a crush on Rachael Ray. One dreadfully slow night, we created *Lechuga Man,* a head of iceberg lettuce, a red pepper nose and mouth, and black beans for eyes. We were *really* bored. As the night progressed, we felt bad for Lechuga Man. He was all alone. So we invented Professor Parsley. We toyed with the idea of writing a kids' book with a whole cast of vegetable characters.

During Brad's first week, the Texas Café got slammed. I wasn't working. Brad suggested that Joan call me to come in. I would have been there in a heartbeat, but Joan screamed that calling me was unnecessary and that I cost too much.

Bringing me in to improve the restaurant's flow that evening would have cost less than thirty dollars. My colleagues and I knew we were in for a wild ride with Joan's uneven temperament and poor decision-making skills. Things at the Texas Café were a'changin'.

MISTAKES OF AN EXPO

To-go orders were bothersome to prepare, especially when the restaurant was busy. Every side had to be wrapped individually when an order of fajitas came through. Separate ramekins were needed for sour cream, guacamole, pico, and cheese. When I first began working as an expo, I sometimes forgot one of the numerous items that were included with a fajitas order.

I typically forgot to include rice and beans, but eight out of ten customers never touched them. However, one of those two out of ten was a woman who regularly ordered fajitas to go. Four ramekins and four tortillas wrapped separately and I was done. We were busy; I took the bag of food to the bar and handed it to the woman. The to-go ticket always went inside the bag so the bartender knew which items were for which people when there were multiple to-go orders.

About an hour later, Joe, the bartender, came into the kitchen. He asked if I forgot the rice and beans for the fajita to-go order. Oops. I was surprised by his response.

"The lady was so upset she came back."

She drove all the way back to complain *in person*. She was letting Joe have it. She demanded to see me. Joe and Devon advised that I remain in the kitchen. Apologies were offered.

With a lethal combination of liquor and tobacco on their breath, the bar regulars reenacted her fury, "Where! Is! That! Motherfucking *son of a bitch* with glasses?"

The regulars howled as each one did his own impression of the crazed lady.

She continued to come in, but I made sure someone else delivered her food. Everyone got their rice and beans after that.

Meghan, Milton, and Devon understood that people made mistakes. Joan never got that memo.

In the heat of the moment when there were thirty tickets in my window, plates to garnish, and food to run, it was plausible that I had overlooked a "no sour cream" note on a ticket. On the night this occurred, the diner complained to Joan. She stormed into the kitchen, *dropped* the plate at my station, grabbed the ticket, and shouted in my face, "What the fuck does this ticket say?"

The ticket did indeed say, "no sour." No big deal, replate the dish. I was ready to move on, but she wasn't.

"Well then why in the *fuck* is there sour cream on this *fucking* plate?"

Some of my mother's friends came into the Texas Café for dinner. After I ran food to a table, I went over to say hello. One of Joan's new rules banned me from the dining room (with the exception of my running food), but I figured there would be no harm in my greeting guests.

Joan came over and shouted, "Ken! back in the kitchen, now!"

The friends looked up to me, stunned, and said, "Well ... tell your mother we say hello."

SUNDAY BRUNCH

If you're not a morning person and you hate chaos, you will understand why Sunday brunch was the worst time to work with Joan. Everything was going smoothly. Suddenly, the kitchen door burst open, and Joan stormed in. The door hadn't closed when she began screaming.

She took her frustrations out on me. At that point in my employment, I had no idea that the expediter's duties included making sure the kitchen was running smoothly and the cooks were coordinating their times. I was only doing what I had been shown.

Joan asked about a salad for table fourteen. Sure enough, there was a salad in the window. This was before the carbon copy system had been implemented, so I had no idea if it was fourteen's. Before I could ask the cooks, Joan and the salad were on their way to table fourteen. But the folks at table fourteen had ordered a *different* salad. A few seconds later, Joan was back in the kitchen and furious.

"Hey *asshole,* you gave me the wrong *fucking* salad!"

In one swift motion, she threw the plate, salad and all, into the garbage can and told the cooks to prepare the right salad. That was a good idea ... now someone else's salad needed to be remade.

That wasn't the only thing that got remade. Joan announced with great pleasure that she would be getting breast implants. She was gone for two weeks to recover and returned during Sunday brunch, her "favorite" shift of the week. She waved me down as soon as I walked into the crowded dining room and pointed to her chest. We hoped that she would accidentally knock something over or hit a customer in the face with her new additions.

STOLEN VODKA

As odd as this may sound, I owe Joan a lot. I learned a lot from her, especially regarding who can and cannot be trusted. When a bottle of vodka went missing during Diana's bartending shift, Joan accused Diana of stealing it. According to Joan, she and Diana were the only people with the key to the liquor cabinet.

Diana was outraged. If you saw her on the street, the Double A battery that she used as an earring might make you think twice about her. But Diana wasn't dishonest. Nevertheless, she received a written warning. Joan told her the next time liquor went missing, she would be fired.

At the end of the night, Diana went into the manager's office to get extra bar towels. We weren't surprised when Diana ran downstairs and told us the vodka was under Joan's desk. Diana talked to Bob, the regional manager, who did nothing.

A few weeks later, the tension at the Texas Café was so thick, breathing was hard. There was talk about a walkout. Bob came in at the height of the tension. He was hardly a foot in the kitchen door when I stopped him and told him we needed to talk.

I told Bob that it was imperative that he do something about Joan. Working conditions had become unbearable. There was no way we could continue to work with her.

Bob assured me he would talk to her. He also told her that I was the one who complained. Joan despised me from that moment, and their talk accomplished nothing.

MORE MONEY

My illustrious career at the Texas Café was going strong. I was doing far more than my original job description, and $8.50 an hour wasn't cutting it. I asked Joan for a raise. She said she could give me a raise on the date of my one-year anniversary.

My one-year anniversary was a month away. Joan told me she would love to give me the dollar raise I had requested but would have a hard time convincing the corporate office. If I did something else in addition to my current job, she could "convince them with ease."

The something else turned out to be cooking one day a week. I liked cooking and had paid attention to the cooks' work for months. Deal.

I then found out I got the dollar raise to expo but my pay rate remained at $8.50 an hour to cook. Less money for a more difficult job? If I had been more confident, I would have requested $9.50 for both tasks. I later discovered Joan could give me a raise on her own authority. So what was all the talk about the corporate office's approval? I wasn't sure, but I was going to find out.

Joan insisted I needed training, and so my one additional shift as a line cook suddenly turned into three shifts.

All the pieces of the puzzle fell into place. Armando, one of the line cooks, was taking a two-week vacation. So that's the reason Joan wanted me to cook! She delayed my raise until October because she knew Armando would be on vacation then. She didn't want me cooking in September because that would have been a waste of money. Her intention was for me to be his replacement with two weeks' training. There was a reason behind her deception; she wanted me to be prepared.

A week into Armando's vacation, Melvin, another line cook, *also* went on vacation. I was now covering for him as well.

I was cooking every weekday morning and expediting Thursday, Friday, and Saturday nights, and Sunday morning. Not only did I get zero days off, I got my first taste of the double shift. I cooked from 8 to 3 PM, ate lunch, went to the gym, and returned to work from 5 to 11 PM.

Meanwhile, we were running out of line cooks. Joan promised that I would never cook solo, but I knew her promises were unreliable. Luiz, who was responsible for catering, was asked to help me cook. Every morning at eight, Luiz and I would meet in the kitchen and figure out how two rookies could have the restaurant up and running by eleven. A few weeks into my new job as a line cook, I was teaching Luiz how to set up the line. Luckily, he knew how to prepare the dishes that were on the catering menu.

It was time to talk to Joan. I was furious about the situation and told her it was not what we had agreed on. It didn't take an idiot to realize I was pissed off, so Joan tried to resolve the issue. She told me I could stop cooking entirely once the cooks returned from vacation. I agreed. Two more weeks of this bullshit and I was done.

The sad reality is, while I complained about cooking that I had volunteered to do, a lot of employees, legal and otherwise, have no choice but to work unspeakable hours to support their families. I was physically and mentally worn thin after the double shifts and could not imagine how I'd feel if I had to work like that every day. This schedule was an opportunity to see how people struggle *barely* to get by.

Devon left the Texas Café around this time and was replaced by Richard, who had worked at another Texas Café location. Joan introduced us by saying, "This is Ken. He's the expo, but he's also helping us cook for the next few months while the cooks are on vacation."

Furious again, I insisted on more money if I was going to be cooking longer than two weeks. Joan promised that once I got the "hang of things" I would get a raise. I was working seven days a week with double shifts four days in a row. I was cooking, expediting, *and* training Luiz. What else was there for me to get a hang of? I never did receive the raise under Joan's watch.

Remember the promise that I would never be alone on the line? Luiz was usually on time, but at eight one morning, Luiz was nowhere to be found. Joan told me he was in the hospital with his girlfriend, who had temporarily lost her vision.

That Joan was managing that morning only made matters worse. I had been screwed into a miserable position. Enough was enough; it was time for a change. The second she raised her voice to me, I got a chance to stick up for myself.

"If you yell at me again, I will leave this instant."

Joan realized the Texas Café needed me more than I needed the job. I did the best I could considering I was a relatively new cook flying solo during a jam-packed lunch crowd.

Eventually all the line cooks returned from their much-needed vacations, but I continued to cook two days each week. It was extra money, and I wasn't alone on the line.

Chapter Three

A Roach's Kitchen

Here is the segment you don't want to read. This is about the aspect of the restaurant business you wish you could ignore—rats, roaches, filth, and grime. It ain't pretty.

One thing I admired about White Spice was how strictly its staff enforced cleanliness. I never saw a roach or rat, not even outside. The kitchen was cleaned—really scrubbed—twice daily. The only bug I ever saw was a huge black widow spider that came in with a vegetable shipment.

The same can't be said for the Texas Café. While the kitchen was cleaned nightly, the cleaning was a cursory once-over. When I eat out with friends and family, they ask me not to voice my concerns because they don't want their meal ruined. Sometimes, I can't help it. If I see something in the dining room that shouldn't be there, I wonder what's going down in the kitchen.

DRESS TO IMPRESS

Appearance at a five-star restaurant is critical. Shaving is mandatory. If I didn't shave at White Spice, my job was threatened. I shaved, tucked in my shirt, ironed my pants, and combed my hair. If I neglected one of those items, the GM's lecture ended with "or else you're fired."

Things were different at the laid back Texas Café. Rules were minimal. For instance, Jared was the kind of waiter who would sit down at a table to take an order. If customers didn't mind Jared's approach, I doubt they were concerned about a tucked-in shirt. None of the managers had ever enforced that rule. Even Joan didn't care about shirts.

Similarly, I never worried about shaving. Customers weren't outraged by stubble, so why bother? If I was cooking, appearance mattered even less.

I arrived at eight one morning to set up the line. I was chopping onions when a strange man walked in. Since food purveyors were in and out early in the morning, I figured he was one of them. He came up to me, patted me on the back, and in an incredibly condescending tone of voice said, "Yeah, next time, try shaving, okay *buddy?*"

I looked at him in shock and said, "Who the hell are you?"

I nearly had a stroke when he introduced himself as the president of the company.

The Latino guys had stubble on their faces as well, but they got no lecture. He probably assumed white guy equals waiter, not cook.

Later, another stranger approached me in the kitchen. She got right up in my face and shouted, "Hey! Tuck your damn shirt in!"

After my run in with the president, I had learned my lesson. I asked politely who she was. She responded, in a snotty, holier than thou voice, "I'm *Rachael!*"

Her name meant nothing to me. She rudely explained she was the Bethesda Texas Café Manager.

"You had better tuck your shirt in!"

She left the kitchen and proceeded to scream at Devon about my improper attire. She could have introduced herself and explained politely that tucking your shirt in was corporate policy. I guess that would have been too easy.

Devon's observation about eating with your eyes first can be applied to restaurants' dress codes. If everyone appears clean and presentable, it follows that the restaurant is clean as well. A great illusion.

OH, RATS!

In the fall of 2003 we had a mini rodent epidemic that started with a frightening discovery. A rat was dying after eating a poison pellet. He decided to drag his ass right outside the back door to his final resting spot.

The problem was, we were out of tortillas, which were stored in the outside walk-in. Someone had to go outside. The cooks and waiters wouldn't. Call me a wimp, but I'm not stepping over a giant, fidgeting rat gasping for air. Joan had bigger balls. She got the tortillas, came back into the kitchen, and threw them at me.

"There are your *fucking* tortillas!"

NIGHT SQUIRRELS

One night Ryann, a waiter, went to the parking lot to throw away some boxes. Moments later, she screamed and ran back into the kitchen shouting, "I stepped on one! I stepped on one!"

The rodent problem was terrible. In the parking lot, one of the neighboring restaurants owned a large tool shed used for storing wood for brick-oven pizza. It was dark, damp and cool … the perfect home for a rat. Management finally called the exterminator. Poison pellets were placed strategically throughout the lot.

When the exterminator arrived on a busy Thursday night, I realized that a huge and foolish mistake had been made. Who arranges for an exterminator to come through the dining room during the dinner hour? In walked this big dude who *looked* like he killed rats for a living. A very noticeable tube of peanut butter stuck out of his duffle bag. This guy wasn't here to fix no sink.

I took him outside (why didn't the manager do this?) to show him an abandoned oil tank behind the Texas Café where I thought the rats were living. Finally, the exterminator looked at the kitchen. He told me that in his eighteen years in business, he had never seen a rat in a kitchen. I figured that was a joke he used to rile us up before he pulled out a dead rat and said, "Guess you're the first."

On his knees looking under our equipment, he explained, "The digested poison pellets rapidly dehydrate rats. That's why you don't smell 'em."

Customers aren't stupid. They see a fridge being moved and hear kitchen employees gasping in unison and shouting, "Ewwwwww!"

Roaches had come to feast on the rat that had chosen the refrigerator as a good place to die. Had they crawled into the fridge? Probably.

Hank, the manager who had replaced Milton, came into the kitchen *just* as the exterminator was removing the rat from under the fridge. In the midst of this horror, Hank kept the door open to give the exterminator some more room.

Up to that point, I had never raised my voice to a manager, but Hank got a piece of my mind in a loud whisper.

"Close the fuckin' door!"

"Why?"

He stood there offering the customers a clear view of Rat Disposal 101.

Dead rat number two was found baking under the oven. At 9 AM the oven was turned on and set to five hundred degrees. It was turned off at midnight. Food isn't the only thing that cooked in or around the oven.

A third dead rat was discovered under the sink. Water splashed and leaked around the sink, so it was no surprise that water found its way onto the floor. Water also found its way onto a mold-covered rat.

While the exterminator was removing the rats, he explained that rodents were capable of scaling walls. On the kitchen's roof, rats had discovered a hole that led inside. Sure enough, a day later, a rat fell through the hole on a prep cook's head.

The kitchen wasn't the only Texas Café rat graveyard. A bartender noticed that the bar's plasma TV wires were chewed and frayed. Rats were in the wall and elsewhere too.

A manager decided to clean out the air vents in the dining room. He was stunned to find eight dead rats in the vents. We had been breathing air that had passed over dead rats. Unsettling? Yeah, a little.

Joan was no fan of spending money but for some reason she splurged on a huge, unnecessary outdoor metal trash compactor. Santos dropped a bag of trash in the compactor and turned it on. It was full of garbage, but that wasn't all. When the metal ceiling lowered, Santos called us outside and shouted, "Escuche! escuche!" We listened to the cries of rats being crushed to death.

RAIN STORMS

Like food shortages or intoxicated coworkers, natural disasters can also make the restaurant world a living hell. A thunderstorm might not seem like much of a natural disaster, but when the drain outside the kitchen exit is clogged (probably with a dead rat), a storm can cause major problems.

Dirty rainwater rushed under the kitchen door and into the kitchen. For some reason, management decided to deal with a flooded kitchen every time it rained instead of fixing the drain.

The problem with a flooded kitchen (besides the obvious) is that cleaning it takes hours. During one torrential downpour, the kitchen flooded so badly that water was getting into places that hadn't been cleaned in twenty years.

I turned to the dishwasher and pointed to something floating in the murky water. Floating around the dead roaches, old food, and dirt was a mysterious object covered in green mold.

"Hey ... *que es?*"

He giggled and called for the others to come look. Manny, a line cook, took one look at the mold-covered object and yelled, running for his life, *"Ay Papi! Una Rata! Una Rata!"*

While the staff was busy mopping the floor and using a water vacuum, we had to turn away customers. It would have been cheaper to fix the drain.

A ROACH'S KITCHEN

Roaches have been around for three hundred million years, so my guess is: They're not going anywhere soon. Still, a creature that doesn't belong in the dining room is enough to ruin a meal. If you see a roach in the dining room, you know what's in the kitchen. It's not what I see that scares me; it's what I don't.

I spotted a big mother of a roach skittering toward a table of women who were all wearing sandals. A master of the poker face, I opted to not freak out. But, unsure of what to do, I stood watching in disgust as the roach disappeared under the table. Did it crawl into a purse that was on the floor?

A young couple ate brunch at the Texas Café every Sunday. I placed their orders on the table. The woman looked at me and calmly said, "Uh ... there's a roach in my food."

I excused myself with her plate and ran back into the kitchen, grabbing Brad on the way. I pointed to the plate. By this time, the roach was enjoying its meal. Brad shrieked and knocked the plate out of my hand and into the garbage can. Amazingly, the couple reordered their breakfast and ate everything.

DON'T KILL ME

Fajita tortillas were placed in a small, circular plastic container. I was pretty sure those containers weren't supposed to be served to diners if they were overflowing with roaches. Horrified, I dropped the container and shouted, "Oh fuck!"

Santos, a dishwasher with many loose screws, thought the funniest thing would be to grab a handful of roaches and throw them at everyone in the kitchen. I punched him. Later that night, he thought throwing a steak knife at my head would be funny. He missed, but he wasn't done *joking* around.

Moments later, I turned around to discover a chef's knife, capable of cutting through bone, an inch from my throat. Santos shouted, "For you! For you!" as he shook the knife in my face.

The cooks warned me not to tell Joan about the incident.

If I told Joan, Santos would lose his job and kill me. The line cooks tried to talk some sense into Santos. They assured me it would never happen again. I blew off their warning and told Joan, who said she would call the police and have Santos arrested. Instead, Santos was warned.

Santos was dangerous, but he wasn't stupid. He knew I had ratted him out, and for months we were on high alert. Even the El Salvadorian line cooks, who had rough pasts, feared Santos. There were nights when he walked in the back door and we turned our heads expecting him to shoot someone. If I had a dollar for every time I checked my back, I'd have several hundred bucks.

Is It Safe?

After horrifying friends with kitchen stories, I'm always asked, Have you stopped eating out? No.

Here are things I look for when dining out:
1.   Cleanliness of the dining room and bar area.
2.   A proactive staff. If a host, manager, or server picks up a piece of trash from the floor, that's a good sign. If he waits to have the busboy pick it up, that's a bad sign. If servers are lazy in the dining room where their money comes from, imagine what's going on in the kitchen. However, a dirty dining room might mean the front of house staff is lazy; the kitchen could be spotless.
3.   Cleanliness of the staff's attire. Do the waiters care enough to keep themselves neat and clean, or are their aprons treated like dirty rags?
4.   Are kitchen tours permitted? At a chain restaurant, the answer is obvious. A five-star restaurant has a reputation to uphold, and if the staff doesn't want you to see where the magic happens, I'd wonder what they're hiding. If you ask on a whim to see the kitchen and they don't hesitate, that's a good sign.
5.   Quality of the food and decor. If the restaurant has fresh and exotic ingredients, a chef with a reputation, and good reviews, chances are the kitchen is in tip-top shape.
6.   Chain restaurants. I avoid them. The guy working the line is there for a pay check, not to improve the reputation and quality of the place.

Chapter Four

Immigrants' Plight

Marvin bussed tables for five years. He was hoping to secure the appropriate paperwork to bring his wife and children to the United States from Honduras. Not a night went by when he didn't talk about how much he missed his family.

He worked seven days a week, eighteen hours a day, and prized Saturdays when he had the evening off. He bussed tables in the mornings at an upscale café and had thirty minutes to change clothes and get to the Texas Café. He sent half his income home. A percentage of the other half went into savings.

One Saturday night, I was surprised to see Marvin standing on line waiting to be seated. I saw his radiant smile all the way from the kitchen. He was coming in for dinner with his family! To other customers eating dinner or waiting to be seated, Marvin's family was like any other dining out together. But this was a very special moment for his Texas Café colleagues. Here was a guy who came to America to make a better life for his family, whom he hadn't seen in *five* years. I now understood why these guys put up with so much.

Marvin bought an apartment with the money he had saved, furnished it, and bought new clothes for his family. His insane schedule paid off.

Do the owners care about Marvin and his success story? They have no idea who Marvin or their other long-term employees are.

Max had eighteen years at the Texas Café. Armando and Octavio followed with eight years. Bartenders Leo and Sammy worked five years. Karmah and Ryann gave four years. Owners often lose touch with their staff as their businesses grow.

In our time there, we employees learned a great deal about one another's culture, a powerful asset. Our experiences have made us better coworkers, bosses, and perhaps even future business owners. How many people get to work side by side with Marvin, witness the hardships he endured, and see a happy ending?

The Latino guys in the kitchen got a big kick out of watching Americans freak out when a giant roach or rat made an appearance. They told me they were used to living in close quarters with roaches and rats. They thought nothing of seeing one skittering around the Texas Café kitchen. Manny insisted the roaches in his apartment watched TV with him at night.

DEFEND YOURSELF

The Texas Café's Latino employees did not think they had the right to speak up for themselves or complain. They appreciated simply having a stable job. Asserting their rights seemed like a sure way to get fired. Many managers took advantage of this. But the Latino guys were fully aware of what was going on. They had their priorities. They worked for family first, themselves second.

In 1988, the Texas Café opened its doors for business. Max, age seventeen, had just arrived from El Salvador. He took a job as a dishwasher. After several years, he became a line cook. Watching him cook was like watching a professional athlete. He was lightening quick, handled the busiest nights with incredible ease, and never appeared panicked.

On slow nights, I felt something hit me every time my back was turned to Max. Black beans. We progressed to volleyball. It kept us occupied for *hours*.

Max noticed something questionable on his hourly print-out. A few nights prior, the restaurant had been very busy and closing side work took thirty minutes longer. Those thirty minutes had been deducted from his total work hours. He didn't understand.

I urged Max to speak to the manager, Carl. If he didn't, Carl would continue to take advantage of him. I explained to Max that Carl thought he wouldn't be observant enough to notice that thirty minutes had been docked. Max decided to give Carl the benefit of the doubt.

A week later, Max clocked in ten minutes early. Max didn't clock in to goof off; he went right to work. The extra minutes were docked. As soon as Max saw that his time had been tampered with, he told Carl he knew what was happening and wanted it to stop. It did.

Joelle was a nineteen-year-old dishwasher from Honduras. He spoke very little English but was savvy and not afraid to speak up. Other line cooks tried to tell him that it wasn't his place to complain or challenge authority. But Joelle realized management was taking advantage of him. He was paid less than seven dollars an hour to wash dishes, clean floors, and mop up cow blood and raw chicken slime from the walk-in fridge. He asked for a raise and was denied. Joelle quit. He found a more profitable job as a construction worker.

BREAK IT DOWN: JOBS NO ONE WOULD WANT

At the end of the night, the line cooks and dishwashers had to break down the kitchen. Food that couldn't be reused the next day was thrown away or taken home. Reusable foods like sauces, cheeses, and enchiladas were wrapped in plastic and refrigerated. Once the food was put away, the line cooks and dishwashers cleaned the entire line and the cooking equipment, washed the walls, mopped the floors—the whole *megillah.*

Cleaning the flat-top grill at the end of the night involved pouring a harsh chemical called D-Greaser onto the scorching-hot metal. The D-Greaser broke down stains that had been baked on, but it also created a hellacious sizzling sound when it hit the grill.

You wouldn't want to inhale it on a nightly basis. One whiff made your eyes burn. Imagine what it does to your lungs. No masks were provided.

I owe the Texas Café a lot. I'm not some ignorant American who thinks Latinos are lazy. They sure as hell aren't. If you perform a job that has been socially deemed as "their" job, you quickly develop respect for their work ethic.

Latino immigrants want to come to America so much that they'll do the most tedious, laborious, and back-breaking work for very little money. The privilege of working in this country and receiving a paycheck is what matters to them.

When they come from a place where they earn 60 cents a day to stitch soccer balls, I suppose $7.50 an hour to clean dirty plates is a major improvement. They take jobs that few Americans want: picking up trash, cleaning up vomit, and mowing lawns. They deserve respect and appreciation. Instead, we have disdain for them without fully understanding their values and culture.

Octavio used to say to me, "We're people, too. It would be nice if the managers shook our hands and asked how we were whenever they came in."

Max was most offended when managers acted nice only when they needed something.

At the beginning of each shift, we shook hands with one another and asked how we were doing. How easy it would have been for management to extend this courtesy to their employees, but they didn't.

Chapter Five
Boost Business?

Even a successful restaurant like the Texas Café had quiet nights. Anything from good or bad weather to terrorist alerts could keep people home. Perhaps the dining public just wasn't in the mood for Tex-Mex that night. Maybe we lost customers to restaurants that offered outdoor seating.

In the corporate restaurant world, a manager can be fired if sales are down. But you can't *make* people come to your restaurant. You can entice them by offering a free appetizer or drink. You can try to appeal to certain age groups. But the bottom line is: if they ain't comin', they ain't comin'.

In July 2004, I presented Joan with eight ideas to improve our sluggish summer business. She ignored them. When Richard arrived to replace Devon, I presented my ideas to him. Joan was still the GM, but I figured showing the ideas to other managers wouldn't hurt.

Richard liked some ideas and provided constructive criticism for others. He assured me he would suggest them to Joan again.

IDEAS TO IMPROVE TEXAS CAFÉ BUSINESS

1. Customers will receive a 10 percent discount if they purchase Texas Café T-shirts and wear them when dining here.
2. Offer taster treats on the sidewalk before dinner hour for neighbors who are deciding where to eat.
3. Tuesday is Family Night. Get 15 percent off your bill.

Advantage: Making this a regular event may attract more families on a night that is typically quiet.

4. Motivate staff with encouragement, praise, and modeling team work, with salary increases as appropriate.

Advantage: Staff feels more committed to the Texas Café. Will work diligently and carefully.

5. Take out an ad in local newspaper—offer 10 percent off when customers bring in the ad.
6. Distribute Texas Café punch cards to customers. When each letter in TEXAS CAFÉ is punched, the price of the meal is reduced by $10.

Advantage: Brings in return customers who like a deal and creates new customers.

7. Host a political event for John Kerry. On a specified night a $25-minimum donation at the door includes free appetizers and one round of drinks; once customers are in, they might order dinner.

Advantage: A Texas-themed restaurant supporting Kerry? This screams publicity. The *Washington Post, Washingtonian,* and local TV news stations might cover this local story. (Notify media two weeks in advance to hype story. Kerry's headquarters in D.C. will work closely with us.)

I can see it now:

"Find out which candidate this local Tex-Mex restaurant is supporting for president on the ten o'clock news."

"This local Texan restaurant isn't supporting Texan George W. Bush for reelection. See who it is supporting at ten!"

8. Price-Fixed Meals: an appetizer, main course, and dessert offered daily throughout the summer.

Advantages: Will entice new and repeat customers *and* will allow customers to sample a wide variety of dishes they might not otherwise order.

Richard had concerns about a few of the ideas. Number two wouldn't work because the Texas Café didn't own the land outside the restaurant. Getting a permit to distribute food there would take more time and effort than it was worth.

He wasn't a fan of number seven either. He thought George W. Bush was a moron, but if we supported one candidate for president, we might offend some diners.

The remaining ideas were good ones, but nothing ever came of them. They would have cost little to implement and might have attracted new diners.

Business was bad. I was trying to help, but I think Joan was offended by a lowly employee offering suggestions for improvement.

BEST BUSINESS BOOST

The best idea to boost business at the Texas Café would have been the removal of Joan. Joan suddenly made a blockbuster announcement. She was getting married in January 2005 and moving to Baltimore, Maryland! She would remain with the corporation at its Baltimore location.

In December 2004, Joan left our location after eight miserable months. She was finally gone. Under her rule, more than a handful of fantastic employees had quit.

FLEX THOSE GUNS

I decided to try a third time and presented my ideas to improve business to Carl. Another idea had been added to the list.

Top Rope Fitness was located across the street from the Texas Café. I suggested that Top Rope Fitness members show their membership cards for 10 percent off their Texas Café meal. In return, we would cater a meal for Top Rope Fitness employees once a month. Carl loved the idea but didn't move on it.

I was tired of suggesting ideas that might boost business only to see them fall on deaf ears. I took charge. The GM of Top Rope Fitness loved my idea. I printed some fliers and put them in the gym's locker rooms. I told Carl that the fliers were up and that he'd better put the discount button on the computer before diners came in that night.

Five months later, Carl had not catered a meal for the gym staff as promised. Top Rope Fitness made an alternative suggestion. The membership consultant asked Carl to donate Texas Café gift cards. The gym would give them to members.

The Texas Café/Top Rope Fitness promotion was a smash hit. It brought in four hundred dollars in sales during the first week. That might not seem like a lot, but the average meal at the Texas Café cost under twenty bucks. The people using the promotion might have been new diners or returning customers. Who cares? The idea was working. However, the waiters weren't so keen about this promotion. Unfortunately, many diners who receive a discount tip less.

A woman came into the Texas Café for dinner with a group of friends. She had intended to use her Top Rope Fitness membership card but had left it at home. She told Carl, the GM, "I really wanted that discount. Is there anything I can do?"

He responded, "How about this. If you flex your muscles, I'll give you the ten percent off."

She rolled up her sleeves and flexed. Other diners overheard this exchange and asked if *they* could get a discount for flexing. Before we knew it, every customer's biceps were flexed.

YOU'RE FIRED

A bartending magazine named Aaron, a Texas Café employee, its Bartender of the Year. Aaron was a bartender with a loyal following. His artwork was displayed throughout the restaurant. Whenever I mentioned to people that I worked at the Texas Café, someone inevitably asked whether Aaron still worked there.

I arrived one morning to find two blank spots on the wall. The Bartender of the Year article was gone. So was Aaron's artwork.

He had been fired.

I thought the line cooks were joking when they told me. Karmah, in tears, confirmed the news. The night before, Aaron and Richard had had an altercation.

A customer had come in to pick up a to-go order. I had left, and no waiters were available to prepare the order. Aaron asked Richard to prepare the order because he was busy, but Richard insisted that Aaron get the order himself. An argument ensued, and the two men ended up in the kitchen shouting at each other.

The next morning, Aaron came in to apologize for his behavior but never got the chance. Carl and Richard had agreed to fire him. That was a critical mistake. An *employee* can be replaced, a *personality* cannot. Aaron knew every customer's name, his hobbies, his taste in music and movies, and what he liked to drink.

Three managers, all in their forties with college degrees, didn't weigh the pros and cons or think of the consequences. When a regular customer comes in and requests a certain waiter, he finds comfort in seeing the same face.

When Aaron was fired, the bar regulars stopped coming. Some wrote angry letters.

I thought of Santos. After threatening to kill me, he remained employed. He was rehired after being fired for drug use. He finally got fired after showing up forty-five minutes late and drunk. The managers had given Santos three strikes before he was finally gone. Santos didn't have a loyal customer base like Aaron. To add insult to injury, Aaron was banned from visiting the restaurant for six months.

JOAN IS FIRED!

We were hugely relieved that Joan no longer worked at our location, but we still wanted her fired. Once she arrived at Baltimore, she managed to get sloppy drunk and fall off a bar stool. The employees were shocked. They organized a meeting with the corporate office to complain.

I had wanted to do the same thing, but my colleagues were afraid of the repercussions. I thought that if twenty employees presented a list of complaints, corporate management would have no choice but to take action. How likely would they be to fire *every* one of us but keep the person who was causing problems?

Joan was finally fired. But in the process, Jared, Diana, Tim, Joe, Deena, Amy, Brendan, and Lily—all great waiters and bartenders— had quit because of her.

Little did I know that, later in my Texas Café career, I would wish for her return.

Chapter Six
Bad, Bad Managers

What constitutes a good restaurant manager? Intelligence, reasonable thinking, no nonsense, and a lack of drama are a few characteristics I would have loved in any one of my managers. Organizational skills help, too. With very few exceptions, most of my managers didn't possess these qualities.

SPLIT PERSONALITIES

Joan didn't know how to motivate staff through encouragement. She lied instead. To get food to a diner faster, she told us the diner was furious about waiting. Her motivational tool? "Customers are pissed." All that did was upset us. The line cooks hustled and rushed to get the food out; I ran it to the diners. When I apologized to them for the delay, they were polite but seemed clueless about my apology.

Joan gathered the waiters in the kitchen for a pre-shift meeting and excitedly announced a contest: "Whoever sells the most margaritas tonight will get a gift card to Best Buy or Barnes & Noble!"

She never delivered.

Joan's furious tirades served as an education. I learned how to speak to an unstable personality not knowing whether "fun Joan," "furious Joan," or "drunk Joan" would respond. I was stunned by her dramatic change in character when the night was over. During business hours, she was harsh, demanding, and rude, but after hours she was fun to be around. The general manager at White Spice also became friendly at the end of the night, cracking jokes and talking about pro wrestling.

On my nineteenth birthday, Joan surprised me by coming into the kitchen with the entire staff. She had a fancy chocolate raspberry cake, complete with candles. We were very busy, but she took the time to rally the staff to sing happy birthday and gave me a hug and kiss.

"Happy Birthday, Ken. Now get the *fuck* back to work!"

I invited my friend Ben to a staff member's going-away party. Ben was eager to meet Joan to see if the horror stories about her were true.

The restaurant had closed, and Ben and I were waiting for Diana, the bartender, to finish her side work. I got Ben a drink, and we sat at an empty table. Diana called us over to keep her company. Ben and I momentarily left the table and drinks behind. On our way to the bar, Joan shouted, "Hey! Kenny's friend!!"

Ben stopped like a deer in the headlights.

"Are you gonna put your glass away, or am I gonna have to bus the damn table for you?"

Ben had hoped to see Joan's outlandish behavior, but he never expected to be its target!

EARNING A BAD REPUTATION

Last I checked, getting fired was only cool if it was by Donald Trump. Richard, one of the better managers, had a reputation for firing employees after their first offense.

On his second night on the job, Richard fired Santos for strolling in forty-five minutes late, smelling of weed and liquor. Santos lurked in the dark parking lot, pacing, all night. Richard began to worry and asked if Santos was crazy. When I told him about the incident with the chef knife, Richard freaked out and asked why no one had told him he was dealing with a lunatic.

"Is he going to wait outside all night?"

"Probably."

"Shit. Is he going to stab me when I walk to my car?"

"Probably."

"Shit! Should I call the police?"

"Probably."

Santos left when he got word that Richard was calling the police.

During a massive snow storm, Gomar, a busboy who commuted from Virginia, decided a car accident wasn't worth the risk. The night before the blizzard's arrival, Gomar told Richard he would not be in if the weather got worse. On the busiest night we had seen in two years, Gomar was absent, as he had warned. He was suspended for three weeks. Was this high school?

The firing of James, a waiter popular among women, stemmed from a party he had attended the previous night. He slipped and cracked his skull open and was discovered unconscious in a puddle of blood. He was rushed to the ER, where his skull was stapled. For some idiotic reason, James came to bartend the next evening. He took a shot of whiskey to calm himself down. His speech became inarticulate, and his last night at the Texas Café culminated in his throwing up at the bar.

A great waiter can convince customers to order extra food and drinks. James was knowledgeable and smart about the business. Unfortunately, Richard gave him an ultimatum: "Get treatment or you're fired."

James didn't seek help. He was fired.

NEW MANAGEMENT, NEW (STUPID) RULES

Many workers think the handbook is a pain in the ass. However, if you own a growing business and have a vision of how it should be run, a handbook may be the most effective way to ensure that things are being done according to your expectations, especially when a business gets too large to attend to each restaurant individually.

But local managers should have room to make judgment calls. For example, if an employee handbook says, "Do not spit in the customer's food," then that's probably a fixed rule. If the handbook says, "Shirts must be tucked in," then that could depend on the restaurant's culture.

The great thing about a neighborhood restaurant is the ability of waiters and diners to interact. On slow nights, waiters pulled up a chair and chatted with their customers. One of our managers insisted that Brad and Dan wear aprons. Had she asked, they would have told her that management's guidelines on uniforms were laid back. Waiters wearing aprons wasn't critical to the restaurant's success.

Authorizing a manager to bend some rules can increase trust between employees and bosses. But when managers enforce every single rule, they alienate the staff. A breach between managers and staff results in pissed off employees who are less willing to lend a hand when needed. Customers have to be happy, but so do employees. Instead, some managers worshipped the corporate handbook as if it were the Bible.

New managers also changed rules without learning how the restaurant ran and imposed new rules to show that they were in charge. They wanted to look productive. They should have assessed the restaurant's culture first.

Joan took away employees' privileges to drink at the bar after their shift. She thought it was inappropriate for diners to see waiters having a beer. (This from a manager who was drunk half the time.) In theory, I agreed, but the Texas Café wasn't some fancy place.

She told employees we could no longer take our meals home because kitchen staff at another location had stolen some steaks and fish. If I wanted dinner I had to eat there. But by the end of my shift, the last thing I wanted to do was spend more time at the Texas Café.

We had a chat. She agreed to my objection but insisted on checking our to-go boxes to make sure we weren't stealing.

Along with enacting new rules, new managers liked to move things around. They thought the restaurant would run more efficiently after they relocated certain items. A new kitchen manager disregarded years of efficient kitchen routines and made dramatic changes without input from the line cooks. When we're used to going to a certain place to get something, and suddenly it's been moved without our knowledge, it's frustrating, not efficient.

Alex eventually achieved his goal of becoming the general manager. He wanted to make an immediate impact by redesigning the upstairs dining room. Diners didn't like eating upstairs because they preferred the camaraderie and energy of the first floor. But because diners love booths, why not move some upstairs? He had good intentions. On the spur of the moment, we took two booths, custom built for a corner, and moved them upstairs. What a hassle. Of course the booths were disproportional and didn't fit. Alex decided to keep them there anyway. The new layout upstairs and downstairs made it impossible to bring trays to certain tables.

Carl, who also took a turn as general manager, was one of the few managers who consulted with his employees before enacting a change. And unlike other managers who may have been embarrassed to admit a lower-ranked employee had a better idea, Carl regularly encouraged and supported suggestions. While most managers wore jeans and a nice shirt, Carl dressed for success: a suit and tie every night.

No Way Out

The Texas Café shared a parking lot with two other restaurants. The agreement was to share this lot for trash can storage and parking. One day the neighboring restaurants asked our managers to stop parking in *their* lot. They claimed we were leaving garbage all over and our employees were taking their parking spots. They erected a wooden blockade outside our back exit, restricting access to the lot. We had to force our trash cans into the small space remaining. This created serious problems:

1. The outside space was limited. It held an ice machine and a walk-in fridge. Now add four huge trash cans. I hated to think that rats had easier access to our walk-in fridge.

2. In order to put trash in the Dumpster, we had to carry trash bags *through* the dining room, outside, around the block, and into the parking lot. Management decided to leave the trash bags in front of our restaurant. Neighbors rightfully complained about the piles of trash. Talk about attracting unwanted customers.

3. With no rear exit or entrance to the kitchen, catering crews and food deliveries were paraded through the dining room.

4. Restaurants are required to have two fire exits. As a result of the blockade, we lost the mandatory second exit. I suggested management call the fire marshal. Surely, he would have the power to make the neighboring restaurants remove the blockade. Without a second quick exit, injury or death could result from a fire in our kitchen. Management decided against that idea. The managers reasoned that no matter what they told the marshal, he would fine the Texas Café. That made no sense to me. *We* were the ones *calling* the fire marshal.

CATERING EVOLVES

Catering was a small-time operation that supplemented the restaurant's income. We were the smallest of the chain's eight locations, so extra bucks were needed. Luiz arrived at the restaurant before the line cooks. He cooked and prepared everything for the catering order. Since we didn't rely heavily on catering income, Luiz could handle one order per day.

When Luiz left, Hank took over. Hank had worked as a manager at our location before. I had trained him on expo, but everything went in one ear and out his other. When I told him to have a shot at the expo line, he stood with a blank look until I realized he wasn't going to do anything. I decided to have him run food. I thought we were on the same page when I handed him a plate of food and told him the table number. He said, "What do I do with this?"

Eventually Joan had Hank transferred to another location. He failed there too and was relocated *again.* Why didn't they just fire him? Now he was back to give catering a try. He always forgot something.

Once it was hundreds of tortillas. Another time, it was twenty-five pounds of beef!

Hank arrived sick and cranky each morning and headed upstairs to nap. He ordered the line cooks to prepare the catering order, handing us a list of items to cook and have ready by a certain time. There's a difference between helping someone do his job and *doing* his job. The line cooks dubbed Hank King Lazy.

With catering fully evolved, corporate realized its mistake in appointing Hank to oversee catering, so he was relocated again (poor guy). Celia was brought in. She arrived with zero regard for how we operated. In her mind, catering came first and everything else could wait. She increased catering orders to an unreasonable eight orders a day.

The cooks were now too distracted to cook for the regular diners. Octavio and Melvin told me they had no problem cooking food for the catering orders when they had time, but they couldn't leave the line to label, package, and prepare the orders.

As a result, diners waited almost forty-five minutes for lunch that normally took fifteen minutes. While Octavio and Melvin were cooking catering orders, I cooked for the diners. The kitchen was built for two cooks, not three. The lack of maneuvering room resulted in some severe burns.

Three weeks into unreasonable requests, neglected lunch customers, and burnt-out line cooks, we were fed up. Would the line cooks complain? Not a chance. They insisted they were lucky enough to be in this country and would do what was asked. It's easy to take advantage of people who are afraid to speak up for themselves. That reason alone is why many business owners, corporate or not, screw their Latino employees.

But just because they wouldn't complain didn't mean that I couldn't.

I told Carl the catering requests were unbearable. Celia never lent a hand. She sat in her office eating McDonald's while we broke our backs to get through lunch service *and* complete her catering orders. Carl arranged a meeting for the back of house (BOH) employees to voice our concerns.

An English/Spanish notice announced a 3 PM meeting in seven days, but Carl "forgot" that most of the kitchen guys worked more than one job. He wanted the BOH employees to take time off from those jobs to attend this meeting. Despite his unreasonable request, Carl was furious when no one showed up for the meeting except the guys who were already working.

Carl stormed out of the room shouting, "I gave them a week's notice!"

The guys on the night shift arrived at 4 PM, and the meeting began. Carl warned that they would be fired if they didn't show up for future meetings. They explained they had other jobs, but he insisted a week was enough warning.

Max, a line cook who had been at Texas Café for eighteen years, didn't show up. He was suspended for two weeks. A stupid decision and a major inconvenience. And Armando was on vacation.

Carl informed us that catering was now our responsibility. We would cook, prepare, box, label, and carry the food to the catering vans. Celia sat in on the meeting but never uttered a word.

As you can imagine, I had lots of questions. Catering had never been our job, I told Carl, and reminded him that Luiz had worked as the caterer. Carl insisted Luiz would have been fired if he hadn't quit because he wasn't booking enough catering events. But catering had been a one-event-per-day operation. If catering was a new responsibility, would we get a raise?

This was supposed to have been our workload all along, insisted Carl. Who was he kidding? Carl's version of events was merely a way to have us take on more duties for the same pay. He said we'd have to prove we were worthy of a raise by working harder. But more money wouldn't give the Texas Café employees super powers. Carl agreed that we already worked as hard as possible. By agreeing, he admitted his flawed logic.

Who would oversee the restaurant orders while we were busy with catering? Carl reiterated that we would have to work harder. What about Celia? If she was in the kitchen to do something like label boxes, that would free up one of us to prepare food for our regular diners. I wanted to know what Celia was doing while we were doing her job.

Carl covered for her. "Celia is busy booking catering events."

Pfft. I didn't buy it. He was clearly taking advantage of us. But unlike most corporate managers, if Carl was doing something wrong, he encouraged us to speak up. I did.

"It's not Richard's job or responsibility to oversee catering orders. But he does. It's not Sammy's job to run upstairs and get catering supplies. But he does. It's not Jose's job to carry catering boxes to a van. But he does. It's not my job to prepare the condiments and box and label them. But I do. You're telling guys who have worked here for twelve years that something they've never done or known about is *suddenly* their job. But while we're doing these *new* jobs, who is cooking the food for the diners? Who is watching the bar? Who is washing the dishes? Who is expediting? We need to get our priorities straight. We're a restaurant first."

Carl insisted that once we worked out the kinks, new employees would be hired.

The meeting came to a close with a moment of massive contradiction. Carl asked, "Well, I need someone to come in next Tuesday and help us with a catering order. Any volunteers?"

Silence.

"Okay. I will pay fifty dollars *cash* to whoever comes in to cook."

I couldn't believe what I had heard. I stood up and said, "You *just* said that you wouldn't pay anyone to help with catering, that we had to *earn* it, and now you're offering fifty bucks? Now every time you ask for volunteers, we'll expect to be paid extra!"

Two line cooks were ordered to come in at 4 AM, four hours earlier than usual. They were instructed to cook and prepare a massive assault of catering orders. Two orders would go out every hour from 8 AM until 7 PM. No special compensation was offered. Amazingly, the entire staff showed up. Not surprisingly, managers were nowhere to be found.

In addition to preparing the catering order, the cooks had to open the restaurant for regular business. The demands were too much for three men to handle. The managers should have shown up to support the staff, but they were busy … sleeping.

I arrived at 8 AM and was stunned to learn that Octavio and Dago had been cooking since 4 AM. I told Carl the hours were criminal. His response showed how clueless he was. "Well, when I worked at the Silver Spring Texas Café, the bar closed at 3 AM, and I normally left by four."

His comparison was insane. For most of those hours, Carl sat in his cushy, air-conditioned office, not standing on his feet, cooking in a smoldering kitchen for twelve hours.

After the morning shift, Celia showed her appreciation by giving me three $10 bills for Octavio, Dago, and Ivar. She told me to tell them, "Thank you."

She hadn't yet given up enough of her responsibilities to employees. She now had *me* thank them for her.

LET'S TALK

Bad managers can be nice people. They can also be disorganized and incompetent. One duty of a manager is to keep track of his employees. At times I told management I wouldn't be able to work a shift only to get a phone call *that night* asking where I was.

My cousin's boyfriend opened a restaurant. I was invited to come in to try out some menu items. The manager was told I'd be coming in and to comp my meal. When I walked in, the manager knew exactly who I was. This seems elementary, but you'd be surprised how little of this kind of communication occurred at the Texas Café.

At the Texas Café, a manager's notebook was supposed to be used to keep track of schedules, problems that arose, supplies that were needed, and so forth. The managers rarely used it. If you had a message for the managers, best to tell them directly *and* e-mail them. Asking one manager to relay a message to the other two didn't work.

Carl told me Armando was going on a two-week vacation the day before he left. Carl needed me to cover Armando's shift four days a week. Employees had to give management three weeks' notice before going on vacation. Wouldn't a good manager arrange for substitutes right away? As it turned out, I was unable to work two of Armando's shifts, and I had planned to be away during my day off the following week.

Caller ID is a terrific invention. I let the machine pick up when I saw Texas Café on the LCD screen.

"Hi Kenneth, this is Carl at the Texas Café. It's Tuesday at 3:30. Just calling to let you know that you will be working tonight at 5 PM. See you then."

Had I heard him correctly? Tuesday was my one day off each week. I replayed the message.

"Hi Kenneth, this is Carl at the Texas Café. It's Tuesday at 3:30. Just calling to let you know that you will be working tonight at 5 PM. See you then."

Okay, I had heard it correctly. I would have been there had he left this message: "Hi Kenneth, this is Carl. Listen, we're in a little bit of a jam, and we're hoping you can come in at five. Sorry for the last-minute phone call. If you can't make it, I understand—but I would really appreciate your help."

His last-minute phone call with demands didn't fly. His tone of voice led me to believe he thought I was just some guy sitting around watching Oprah.

I *was* watching Oprah—in my boxers, eating ice cream.

Another time, management asked me to come in early to lend a hand. The Texas Café liked to get the big catering orders out of the way early in the morning, and, as usual, we were short-staffed. When I arrived, I found Dago, Reuben, and Santos (not knife Santos) waiting outside. Richard was on schedule to work that morning, but not to open. That was Celia's job. The kitchen should have been up and running by eight. I had to call Alex (on his day off) to open the restaurant.

On his way over, Alex called Celia to ask why she wasn't there. She had told Carl three weeks ago that she couldn't work that day, so he needed to be there to open. Carl forgot. Easy solution: a dry erase board with a calendar and comments area. Everyone would be required to check the board on a daily basis so we'd all be aware of the schedules.

On reflection, these events made me think more broadly about running a business. It occurred to me that treating every job as though you were the manager or owner is one way to learn about management. Keep a log of ideas to improve the business. Think about how you would handle a crisis and how you would respond to customer and employee complaints. Consider creating a budget for inventory, wages, and overhead.

Chapter Seven
The Life Of An Expo

My original job description had four requirements. At the beginning of each evening, I stocked the line with everything I'd need throughout the night: to-go containers, pre-portioned containers of fresh condiments including guacamole, sour cream, pico de gallo, cheese, lettuce, and squirt bottles of assorted sauces. Known as *mis en place*, this preparation is essential in a busy kitchen.

Expediting was my primary task.

At the end of each evening I restocked everything I needed for the next night: to-go containers, beverage napkins, and plastic to-go bags. The squeeze bottles of tomato chipotle, chipotle mayonnaise, and sour cream were refilled and chilled overnight.

Keeping the line clean throughout the night was important. If I waited until the end of my shift, the expo line would be a disaster zone. Before clocking out, I thoroughly cleaned the station, which Tim dubbed the KENNY ZONE and labeled with a sticker, and clocked out.

I began to understand how each person's job affected the entire operation. No manager ever told me that I wasn't doing enough or that I needed to do more. While running food helped the waiters, it also gave me a chance to connect with the diners.

Here's what my nights looked like:

1. Set up the line
2. Expedite food
3. Clean up the station
4. Restock the line
5. Run food

6. Wait on tables
7. Refill drinks
8. Take drink orders
9. Restock waiter station and bar
10. Bus tables
11. Host
12. Lend a hand on the line
13. Expo while cooking
14. Run food while cooking
15. Run credit cards

Not everyone enjoys multi-tasking, but I took great pride in accomplishing these tasks. I had done everything at the Texas Café with the exception of management and bartending.

THE BLIZZARD

During the winter months, the Texas Café was practically empty each night. But when the first snow appeared and the weatherman hyped a nasty blizzard, D.C. residents flocked to the Texas Café for their last hot meal. We were caught off guard.

Since we were nearly dead every night of the week, management had reduced the number of employees working per shift. Waiters were paid $2.77 an hour. Management didn't think it was fair to have them commute only to send them home early each night.

The blizzard arrived. With our reduced staff, we were screwed when, for the first time in over two years, we had a wait list. Joan would have been a mess, but I loved it. Everyone had to take on extra responsibilities. Nothing was more exciting.

The next night, with five inches of snow on the ground, who would bother going outside? We were settling in for a slow night, but our predictions were wrong *again*. Diners flocked to the restaurant. There was no host or busboy, only two waiters and a bartender. Texas Café always stressed "teamwork" as if we wouldn't help one another had management not mentioned it. The night was a mess, but the experience was great.

I looked forward to nights when we would be short-staffed in the front of house. No host or busboy? Just bring it! Brad and I worked alone on some nights. He was a pro. He could handle bartending and tables if I took a few tables, bussed, ran food, and expedited.

I remember one night when it was just the two of us. The bar and dining room were full to capacity. We were in trouble. A customer, probably kidding, offered a hand. But when Brad turned to him and said, "Refill the waters!", he hopped to it.

DEMOTE ME!

At times a cook left early. Maybe he was sick or high. I had to be prepared for double duty. Those are the nights I remember as being the most challenging and fun. This happened frequently, yet I was never compensated for performing two distinct jobs.

Sometimes I felt like telling the managers to shove it. Find someone else. But that would have been unfair to whoever was left alone on the line. Unlike management, I thought about my colleagues.

Finally, after Joan left, I asked Carl to relieve me of my cooking duties. Carl had no problem with this. However, the Texas Café was habitually short staffed. I had to fill in. Max's suspension meant I would have to help with the cooking.

Management didn't want to hire an additional cook. I felt strongly about maintaining the restaurant's success. I did what Carl asked. This meant an extra shift from 11:30 AM to 3 PM to help out during this busy time. Think of the money they saved by not having two line cooks in at 8 AM. At least Carl gave me a raise.

Max and Manny, best friends, had cooked side by side for the past four years. I anticipated that I'd be helping Manny that evening, but I should have known that Manny would be outraged over Max's suspension.

Something was up when I walked in that Friday night. All eyes were on me. Alex informed me that Manny had gone home "sick." Lucky for me, Manny had completed the prep work for the night.

Abandoned! And on the busiest night of the week. I was furious with management's rash decision to suspend Max without a replacement and with Armando on vacation.

We had a regular Friday night crowd, but the restaurant seemed even busier. I did the job of two seasoned pros and didn't cut off a finger or burn myself. By the time the restaurant closed, I was covered in sweat, but I felt like the king of the world. What a rush! And ... I never wanted to do it again.

I saw Alex as I was leaving. Like Tommy Lee Jones in *Men in Black*, I held a pen in front of his face.

"Your memory has just been erased. Does Kenneth cook here?" He replied, "Yes."

That trick only works in the movies?

I'M AN EXPEDITER FIRST

New waiters trained one week before earning the waiter title. They followed a waiter, learned how to take an order and put it into the computer, memorized the table numbers, and did menial tasks like retrieving water, chips, and salsa for tables.

They received no tips but got a higher hourly rate during this period. As they progressed, they would be reverse shadowed. A waiter followed his trainee to make sure the new guy was doing everything correctly.

The final step in the trainee program was spending two nights with me to learn my job. Unfortunately, management always insisted I train new waiters on the busiest night of the week. Flawed thinking. Sure, they got to see us at our busiest, but they didn't learn shit.

Trainees were then phased into waiting tables on their own. They served a small section until they were comfortable. Unfortunately, the new guys weren't always so lucky. If a waiter called in sick, new guys found themselves working a jam-packed dining room with little help.

New waiters always asked me to run their food. I'd point to four trays *full* of food and a window stacked with sizzling entrees. They didn't get the picture that I was too busy to run their food.

Finally, they stormed into the kitchen and shouted, "Hey! I *really* need you to run my food!"

I pointed to a window full of forty tickets for entrees that had not been prepared. I don't believe in yelling at people, but sometimes it's necessary. A calm demeanor wasn't going to cut it.

"I *only* run food when I have time! Run it yourself!"

They'd grumble and grab the food, which was now cold. Customers complained. The entrees had to be reheated.

The Problem with Running Food

My duties were in the kitchen. The more food I ran, the more the kitchen got backed up. I'd rush to the dining room hoping to return to the kitchen ASAP. That rarely happened. An average night went something like this:

I dropped off a tray of food at table fourteen. The diners asked for more salsa. On my way to get their salsa, I was stopped by a man at table sixteen asking for another side of guacamole and then a waiter telling me table twelve wanted a small queso. I picked up the salsa for table fourteen and got stopped by another waiter. "Is twenty-three's food ready yet?" Food was coming up in the window as I spoke. I had to get back to garnish everything, but I had to deliver the salsa to fourteen, get the guacamole for sixteen, grab the queso for twelve, and check table twenty-three's food.

I rushed back to the kitchen and grabbed the guacamole for table fourteen ... or was it sixteen? No, fourteen was the salsa. Guac was for sixteen. I ladled out the queso for twelve and then checked the ticket for twenty-three. It wasn't ready yet. Queso at twelve, guac at sixteen. I told the waiter who asked about twenty-three that the food wasn't ready yet.

A guy at table eighteen called me over. He wanted a beer but couldn't find his waiter. No problem. He ordered a Corona, and I picked it up at the bar and dropped it off at eighteen. Twenty-three's food was probably ready. On my way into the kitchen, table twenty-two wanted more water. I couldn't get it. I could see the smoke from the fajitas filling up the kitchen. They had to be sold while they were sizzling or else the novelty aspect of ordering fajitas was killed. Moving like a covert agent, I located a waiter, motioned with my thumb and pinky (like a telephone) to my mouth, and pointed to twenty-two. He got the message: Twenty-two needed a drink. Now he had to add that to *his* to-do list.

Finally, I would hit the kitchen. Twenty-three's food was ready; so was table ten's.

The skills applied here aren't ones you'll necessarily learn in school. Sure, you have to balance your work. You have a test on Thursday, a paper due on Tuesday, an oral presentation on Friday. Those tasks can be planned in advance, but the challenge in the work world is being able to manage three things that need to be solved immediately.

IF YOU'RE GOING TO BE NASTY, CHOOSE WISELY

During my time at the Texas Café and White Spice, I encountered a fair share of jackass diners—and I wasn't even a waiter. It's a wonder more wait staff don't murder some of the diners. At the Texas Café, I had a nice balance of kitchen and dining room experience. I learned to go from one environment to the other in rapid succession without revealing my frustrations.

An expediter or food runner's income isn't dependent on his civility to customers. If a waiter is rude to a customer, he gets a shitty tip. My salary wasn't affected if I was rude. On the other hand, customers might take *my* rudeness out on their waiter and tip poorly.

I ran food to a family with two teenagers. I asked if I could get them anything else. Without looking at me the husband said, "Get me a fork."

I waited for other requests and then went to retrieve his fork. He looked away from me as I put his fork down. No thank you, smile, or head nod. As I left, the wife shouted, "Hey you! Get me a plate!"

Waiters get that shit all the time. It would have been appropriate for me to politely request that she not address me in that tone, but that's not how I rolled. I got her plate, returned to her table, and dropped it in front of her, "There's your damn plate."

Her eyes widened. I returned to the kitchen without looking back. It sure felt good.

THE TIP OUT

At the end of the evening waiters gave a tip out to busboys and bartenders. Fifteen percent of the waiter's total tip went to the busboy and 7-10 percent to the bartender.

I asked management to include me in the waiters' tip outs but changed my mind. An additional 3-5 percent for me wouldn't be fair. If business was slow and a waiter made $60 in tips that evening, giving away 25-30 percent was a hard hit.

Richard came up with a plan. Each waiter would give me $3 each night. With four waiters on any shift, $12 on top of the $9.50 I was earning wasn't a bad deal, and it wouldn't break the waiters' banks. But then Richard said the GM might decrease my pay to $7.50.

The restaurant would pay me less. The waiters would tip me out, which meant they made less. Who benefited? The owners. I declined.

Management tried to alter the tip out. They decided 7-10 percent would go to busboys, and 3-5 percent should go to the bar. Working at $5.50 an hour, busboys depended on those tips. Busboys would receive less in tip outs but would get a $1 per hour raise. If the wait staff had followed management's suggestion, the busboys would lose money—about $100 per week.

EMPLOYEE OF THE YEAR

The honor of winning an Oscar or a Grammy could not compare to the prestige of earning the Texas Café Employee of the Year Award.

The Employee of the Year vote took place at the annual holiday party. We voted on two Employees of the Year, one for back of house and one for front of house. Front of house (FOH) included bartenders, hosts, busboys, and waiters. Back of house (BOH) included prep guys, line cooks, dishwashers, and the expediter.

Voting was underway when Joan arrived. At the time, she was employed at the Baltimore location. Joan saw the list and was stunned to see my name under BOH. My job was BOH according to my job description but not according to Joan. Funny, because as you recall, she screamed at me in front of my mom's friends for being in the dining room.

She demanded my name be moved to FOH. This was her last opportunity to create a problem before she was gone forever. Ryann, the waiter who was collecting votes, and Alex, our manager, didn't give into her. Joan left before the votes were tallied.

In the past, the Employee of the Year won a round-trip vacation to San Antonio, Texas. Dago, the food prep guy, won two years in a row. Would you be surprised if I told you management never delivered his prize?

Ryann announced the results. Karmah won FOH. Yours truly won BOH. Out of forty employees at the party, I received forty votes.

Karmah and I were promised a $200 Visa gift card. We received them ... five months later.

GETTING OLDER AT THE TEXAS CAFÉ

By the time my second birthday at the Texas Café rolled around, Joan was long gone. No cake this year. My high school friends urged me to call in sick and go out with them. I opted for work.

When I walked in, Amanda presented me with a handful of candy and a happy birthday hug. Later, Renay, a bartender/waiter who was off that night, came into the kitchen with the entire staff, cake in hand. Renay felt bad that I was working on my birthday. She gave me a brown paper bag and said, "We know you're only twenty and can't legally buy liquor yet, so we hooked you up."

With sparkling cider.

DRUG DEALS IN THE KITCHEN

Drug use is common in all walks of life, but it seems to be prevalent in the restaurant business. Some employees show up drunk or high on heroin or cocaine. They need an airplane bottle of whiskey just to pull them through the night. They smoke a joint when no one is looking.

Why is drug use so common in this industry? Is it the high stress and demands of the business? Or are users attracted to this work because they think getting drugs will be easier in this environment?

I think there's a third, more obvious reason: cold, hard cash. The more energetic and social you are, the more tips you earn. The more cash you have, the more you can spend on your drug of choice: liquor, weed, or harder stuff.

Drug deals in the kitchen were commonplace at the Texas Café. Sometimes they took place in the walk-in fridge or the parking lot out back. You could usually tell the difference between a cigarette break and a drug deal. The drug deal entailed two employees going out "for a cigarette" and then disappearing for a while; a cigarette break occurred at the back door.

Santos, the dishwasher who tried to kill me, stepped outside one evening. He returned a different person. He was stumbling, mumbling, and could barely support himself. His legs turned into butter in front of our eyes.

He was standing by the stereo with his mouth open. The lights were on, but no one was home. Meanwhile, we had a restaurant to run and dishes to wash. We were simultaneously keeping an eye on Santos to make sure he didn't do something dangerous.

Alex, the manager of the night, came in and told Santos to get ahold of himself. Santos tried, but in the process dropped a stack of plates on the floor. He ran away to hide but instead crouched in the corner and put his hands over his face.

Restaurant employees are the kings and queens of the poker face. When I ran food or made sure everything was running smoothly, diners would have never guessed that I was dealing with a frantic kitchen. There were no clean dishes, broken plates were on the floor, and our dishwasher was tripping. But when we delivered food to a table or took an order, we appeared cool and collected. It takes a *lot* of control to remain calm in a hectic and sometimes hostile environment. Alex fired Santos that night, but Joan rehired him days later. Why? I couldn't tell you.

The day after New Year's, Allen, a waiter, was out of his mind. I arrived early to find the front door locked. Allen was at the bar, so I knocked on the window. He leapt up, looked at me, and gave me the middle finger. He looked overly cautious and alert. His jaw was trembling, and he was covered in sweat. I discovered that he had been up until 4 AM smoking crack. He could barely walk a straight line. Allen did his best that day but was clearly incapable. Props for showing up, though.

James, the popular bartender and waiter, had a little thing for crystal meth and binge drinking. Every night, James escaped through the back exit and chugged an airplane bottle of whiskey. It never adversely affected his job. He was one of the best waiters at the Texas Café. Some people left notes complimenting his service. Women often left their numbers for him.

Diners are unaware of the many reasons food service can be delayed. Some include dealing with an asshole manager, coworkers tripping on acid, or a dishwasher wielding a knife.

CONTROLLED CHAOS

People wonder how working in a small, neighborhood restaurant can involve so much drama. The job involves constant stress and verbal abuse from rude customers, enraged managers, and prima donna chefs.

This is one reason that the restaurant business is a good place to develop self-confidence. If you're shy, waiting on tables and interacting with diners will help develop your skills in listening to, speaking to, and dealing with the tough customers in a productive way. (You don't want to follow my example of dropping a plate in front of a rude customer.) Coping with a difficult manager develops a person's confidence. Becoming a team player will serve you well in whatever career you pursue.

In two years, I went from first-night panic as an expo to loving controlled chaos and drama.

Chapter Eight

Weird Coworkers And Famous Customers

Every student has a teacher he dislikes. In every office there's a boss or coworker someone can't stand. In addition to Joan, a handful of my coworkers were beyond weird. One option was to appreciate their quirks and laugh, but some were so obnoxious we anxiously waited for them to quit or be fired.

ALEXIS ... AND HANK (AGAIN)

Alexis was a bartender and a waiter who was trouble. She had been fired from a previous restaurant for telling a customer to fuck off and go to hell. The manager at her old job was the same person who hired her at the Texas Café: Celia.

One night Alexis told me, "I don't know why everyone hates me. I'm not *trying* to be a bitch. I just say what I think."

I heard Hank would be covering while some of our managers were on vacation. Lucky us. Much to my surprise, he was a new person—in charge and aware of his surroundings. His surroundings happened to include Alexis.

Alexis was in her typical "I hate everyone" mood and was causing problems. She sent in orders that weren't prep sequenced (a computer method used to tell the cooks if a table is ordering appetizers or if a customer requests an appetizer as an entree). As a result, appetizers came out with entrees or, even worse, entrees came out as appetizers. She ran food to the wrong tables and then scoffed at customers who complained about her poor service. Hank asked, "Is she having a bad day, or does she always act like this?"

He was amazed when I told him she was like this every day. Hank sent Alexis home, even though doing so made us short-staffed. He volunteered to help. He had learned that a temperamental employee could cause problems.

At the end of the night, Hank wrote Alexis up in the manager's book, and she was fired soon after. Hank had grown into a capable manager.

SHREK

He wasn't green, wasn't an ogre, and didn't eat bugs. Where did the name come from? Not a night went by when he didn't do something strange that made us laugh. Stand up comedian Dave Attell asked, "You ever make fun of someone so much you think you should thank them for all the good times you've had?"

Shrek claimed to be a bodybuilder. He was 6'3" and 250 pounds, very little of which was muscle. A group of women came in having just finished a marathon. Shrek asked how their run went and commented on their calves. He, too, had big calves. He hoisted his leg onto their table, rolled up his pant leg, and flexed his calf.

When Shrek approached a new table, he greeted them by ringing an imaginary door bell. "Ding Dong!"

But along with his goofy personality, Shrek also had a temper. On his way to the upstairs dining room, his towel snagged a tray and sent it crashing to the floor. He locked himself in the bathroom and shouted obscenities in Italian. If the computer didn't work when he was placing an order, he punched the screen and shouted "Fuck this shit," which could be heard throughout the dining room.

When he wasn't working, he wore a tongue ring, and his tattoos of flaming skulls wrapped in barbed wire were displayed proudly.

JAMES AND ALLEN

By looking at them, you would never know their love for binge drinking and drugs. James wanted to follow in his parents' footsteps as a stockbroker. He would have to wait ten years to pursue his goal because of legal complications. He had served a prison sentence for crack possession.

Allen had a passion for culinary arts. His dream was to be a chef in a five-star restaurant. He attended one of America's top culinary schools: Johnson and Wales. Anthony Bourdain's *Kitchen Confidential* goes into great detail about drug use among chefs and cooks. Allen should fit in just fine.

Even though these two had major issues, they were not the scum of the earth that might come to mind when you think about drug addicts. They were two nice people.

Before Carl arrived at our location, we were warned that he was a practical joker. James arrived with a can of soda to begin his shift. He stepped into the kitchen to get some limes, and when he returned to the bar, Carl shouted, "Damnit, James! you know how I feel about open soda cans at the bar! Chug it or toss it!"

James wasn't about to throw away something he paid for, so bottoms up. A split second later, James sprayed the contents all over the bar. Carl had emptied a shaker's worth of salt into the soda can.

NICOLE

Nicole, shy and aloof, was the weirdest person I'd ever met. Every once in a while she would do something that would cause a moment of awkward silence.

She approached me, put her hand on my shoulder, and whispered, "Ken ... I have a *very* personal question for you."

I prepared myself.

"Is ... is Ken short for Kenneth?"

As soon as she asked, she pulled back, grimaced, and averted her gaze, worried that she had gone too far. She bit her bottom lip, afraid that I was going to lash out at her for asking such a personal question.

"Oh God, I'm sorry! I shouldn't have asked."

That was the easiest personal question I had ever answered.

MANNY

Manny, an El Salvadoran line cook, had a personality with a mischievous bent. On slow nights, he pointed to a nonexistent wrist watch.

"You know, Kencito—is slow tonight, my friend. You know, when is slow, I like to make funny, you know—laughy laughy to make time go shooooh."

If your back was turned to him, he walked by, grabbed your ass, fought back the giggles, and insisted, "Small kitchen, you know? I sorry."

Manny enjoyed spending money. He presented a can of chipotle chilies to Brad, offering him fifty dollars to eat the contents. Brad refused until Manny handed him two hundred dollars. I got a slice of bread for Brad to help absorb the heat. His eyes watered as soon as he opened the can. Brad backed out, but Manny wasn't ready to give up on his quest for entertainment. He pulled out another hundred dollars and handed me a fork. No thanks.

Manny announced that he was leaving the Texas Café to cook at Seafood Palace and told Sammy his news. Sammy stated a fact we all knew. "Oh, you'll be cooking a lot of fish."

Manny looked at him curiously.

"Why?"

Manny was in love with American culture. He used his cell phone constantly and got a new, more advanced phone every month. Every six months, he traded in his car for a new one. He also had a passion for cocaine. When the restaurant got busy, he'd run outside and do a line of cocaine off the bed of his pickup. He would waltz back in nonchalantly. The drug use never adversely affected his work.

Karmah and I teased him, pushing one nostril shut and asking, "A little cocaine, my friend?" He denied it, but then a smirk emerged. He was positive that when he died, God would welcome him with open arms, so he lived every day as if it were his last. Cigarettes? "Who cares if they cause cancer?" he would say.

"Not too much, maybe one or two a day. On my day off, some marijuana, a few *cerveza*. Is okay, my friend, to enjoy life."

Manny asked me to cover for him one Saturday night. We all knew it was his last shift, but he didn't want to work. He insisted, with a smile, that he had to take his nonexistent wife to immigration at eight at night. He assured me he'd be back by 9:30. Just like that, he was gone. He left in typical fashion—making, you know, laughy laughy.

Occasionally, Joan would burst into the kitchen screaming at Manny for something he had done. Instead of apologizing or offering an explanation, he simply donned a blank look and said, in perfect English, "Sorry. I don't speak English."

He'd turn around like a little kid and fight back the laughter. He couldn't contain himself and that, of course, pissed Joan off even more.

NELSON

Nelson was a great dishwasher, no doubt about it, but his odd Scooby Doo laugh creeped people out. He understood that having fun made time fly, so as soon as he clocked in, he became a character. A sign posted out back read: ATENCION, NO MAS URINAR AFUERA.

Or, in English: ATTENTION, DON'T PEE OUTSIDE.

Someone (Nelson) thought, "What's the point of going *all* the way upstairs to use the bathroom when there's a drain pipe right outside?" Now, as you may recall, the outside drain pipes often backed up into the kitchen when it rained.

If only they knew that he decided to *urinar* in the kitchen drain pipe too.

OCTAVIO

I opened the restaurant with Octavio on Sunday mornings. He asked me to arrive ten minutes early so he could include me in the conversations with the prep guys, dishwashers, and busboys, despite the fact that I couldn't speak fluent Spanish.

We arrived before the manager. He made coffee, and we chatted in the dining room. Octavio promptly clocked in at eight, when work officially began. (He didn't want to be paid when he wasn't working.) We headed into the kitchen. Octavio had amazing patience in showing me how to set up the line. He understood that Americans had job stability, something immigrants didn't have. Octavio knew that Americans took time to adapt to a new job, whereas Latinos were determined to work their hardest and do everything right the first day.

One morning I went upstairs to use the bathroom and saw Octavio exiting the women's bathroom. I stopped in my tracks. He was embarrassed. I asked what the hell he was doing. "I just wanted to see what it was like to be a lady—sit down to go pee, you know?"

I told him he could do that in the men's room, but he insisted it wouldn't be the same.

CUSTOMERS

The Texas Café had hosted a handful of celebrities, politicians, and rock stars. George Bush was a fan in the '80s. Melissa Ethridge brought in her entire family. Her waiter was a huge fan. She was so overwhelmed that she came into the kitchen and called her mother to tell her who she was waiting on. "I love her music *so* much! Too bad she's a lesbian and a big-time liberal."

Republicans ...

NEWSMEN AND POLITICIANS

When George Stephanopoulos's wife gave birth to their second child, he was quoted in the *Washington Post* saying the burritos he picked up at the Texas Café the night before were responsible for sending his wife into labor. Management joked that hoards of pregnant women in their ninth month would flock to the Café. I suggested we capitalize on the hype by issuing a press release of our own: Pregnant Women Eat Free. It would be called the Stephanopoulos Special.

I ran into Stephanopoulos a few years later and told him about my idea. He laughed and said, "I would have been all for it!"

Senate Majority Leader Bill Frist and his family came in often. Senator Frist always ordered shrimp fajitas. Normally, the shrimp fajitas came with black beans in case the customer was kosher or a non-meat eater. (The red beans were cooked with bacon.) This shows you the Texas Café's poor knowledge, as kosher Jews refrain from eating shellfish. But I had a feeling Frist wasn't Jewish.

From time to time, we wondered what would happen if Frist and Stephanopoulos were in the restaurant at the same time. Would they get into a heated political discussion? I suggested we host *This Week with George Stephanopoulos* at the Texas Café, interviewing Frist.

Almost a year after I left the Texas Café, Frist came into White Spice for dinner. The instructions from Chef were clear. VIP at table thirty-one—*do not fuck up*. I ran the food, not knowing Frist was dining with his wife. When I got to the table, he looked up at me and said, "Didn't you used to work at the Texas Café?"

Awesome! I chatted with him and his wife about the differences between the Texas Café and White Spice. They asked me which restaurant I preferred working at. I preferred the Texas Café because its atmosphere was laid back. When I returned to the kitchen, Chef was furious. He shouted at me, "Don't talk to the fucking VIPs! Who the fuck are you to talk to the Senate Majority Leader?"

Once Chef cooled down, I told him that I had waited on the Frist family several times at the Texas Café and that Frist had recognized me. Chef smirked, doubting my statement, and said, "Why would Frist eat at a shit hole like the Texas Café?"

"Why don't you ask him?"

Chef shut up once he realized I wasn't kidding. Months later, Frist returned with his family. When his son asked which place I enjoyed more, Frist answered, "You said you liked the Texas Café because it was more laid back, right?"

I informed Frist that I would be leaving White Space. He wished me well. His interest and courtesy were impressive.

PRESIDENTIAL

Max handed me a carbon copy of a ticket for a large to-go order. The names on the order were "Jenna and Barb." I prepared the to-go order and packed it up. When I took it to the bar I noticed a fleet of black SUVs parked out front with security guards. Still, I hadn't registered *Jenna and Barb.*

I called out the names on the ticket, and sure enough, Jenna and Barb took their order, thanked me, and left. On my way back to the kitchen, it hit me that the bullet-proof SUVs were for George W. Bush's daughters.

THE REGULARS

Anyone who has worked in a restaurant can rattle off the names of at least three regulars. They sit at the same bar seat or request the same table. One of my favorite parts of this business was seeing the same faces over and over. If they kept coming back, we must have been doing something right.

We could order *for* them because we knew their preferences. On Thursday nights, we knew to look out for the Queso No Pico Guys. They ordered a bowl of queso to start but didn't like the pico de gallo garnish. Chicken fajitas to share, with extra peppers, came next.

I showed them to their table one night and said, "I'll grab your queso, no pico."

They smiled, happy with the familiarity. Even though the Texas Café was an "evil" corporate restaurant, the regulars lent a small family feel to the ambience.

MIGAS

Audrey visited a few times a week. She ordered the same dish without fail. As a result, we nicknamed her after her entree of choice. She had a routine that consisted of a slightly different prep for her migas.

Scrambled eggs, pico de gallo, tortilla chips, and melted cheese comprised the regular migas. Audrey wanted loose eggs with tomatoes, onions, bacon, no chips, and no cheese. Every once in a while, she wanted a single shrimp on top. Instead of red beans and red rice, she wanted black beans and green rice and a vegetable skewer with two corn tortillas and a large side of butter. The plate had to be scorching hot, dangerous to touch.

New waiters dreaded taking her order and typing it into the computer. Her custom order was too complex, so we simplified things. The line cooks remembered her specific request and even knew her nickname, so her order simply said, "Migas para Migas."

QUESO WITH A SPOON GUY

Queso with a Spoon Guy was a loner. He came in once a week. He started by ordering a large queso dip, but ate the dip with a spoon as if it was soup. No one questioned him. He did this for a year until a customer called him on it one night. Embarrassed, he started using the chips, as intended. One night, I brought him his queso and realized he was spoonless. I offered to get him one, but he snapped, "No! I don't *need* a spoon!"

That was the last night he came to the Texas Café. Too bad, because quirks like his made the place unique.

NEW MOMMIES CLUB

A group of women who had recently given birth decided Wednesday lunch would be their day to get together and chat. *With their babies.* We knew to set up the tables to accommodate them before they arrived. By the time they left, it looked like the Texas Café had been attacked by Cheerios. They knew they had left a big mess, so they tipped well.

WALT

Have you ever seen a drunk high on heroin trying to eat? It's not pretty. Walt always stumbled into the Texas Café late at night, fell into a bar stool, and mumbled to himself until his food arrived. He got more food on himself than in his mouth.

One night on his way to the bathroom, he actually fell *up* the steps. The bartender threw him out when he fell asleep on his bar stool and crashed to the floor.

A roach crawling on the kitchen wall was not uncommon. On one particular evening I caught a glimpse of the largest roach I had ever seen. It was dark red, smoking a cigarette, and had a Bush/Cheney bumper sticker on its back. This is the bad-ass roach your parents don't want you to hang out with.

We watched in awe as this monster crawled into a roach motel on the wall but to our horror, came out on the other side and continued moving with the roach motel on his back!

We called it *el cucharacha tortuga*: the roach turtle.

BACHELOR PARTY

Three guys came into the Texas Café for dinner and announced that one of them was getting married. It was a low-key bachelor party. After a few drinks, the groom told Ryann, his waiter, that he loved her Texas Café tie-dye T-shirt. He offered a trade. "I'll give you my shirt if you give me yours."

She insisted that was a foolish trade because she wouldn't wear a man's shirt. I told him I'd take his shirt. Ryann wasn't happy with that. I gained a shirt, the guy got a shirt, but she lost a shirt. What was in it for Ryann? He gave her twenty bucks.

Ryann ran upstairs to get a new Texas Café T-shirt. (The tie-dye ones had been discontinued.) The guy assured me his beautiful button-up, short-sleeve shirt was a chick magnet.

A few weeks later, I wore the shirt on the Vamoose Bus to Manhattan. On the way out of D.C., I spotted Ryann out for her early morning jog. I wanted to shout that I was wearing the shirt that was a guaranteed lady killer. The funny thing was, the guy was right. His shirt *was* a chick magnet. A woman on the bus looked at me and said, "That's a *really* nice shirt."

Too bad the woman was seventy years old.

Chapter Nine

Be Nice To Those Who Touch Your Food

I'm amazed by rude customers. See if you recognize yourself in some of these examples.

Some people are aware of the fact that they're rude so they tip more to compensate for their behavior. That's pretty poor thinking. Any number of things could happen to your food before you leave a nice tip to compensate for your shitty attitude. Your server has direct contact with your food. If you have to complain, be advised to do so *after* you get your food.

Waiters at the Texas Café joked about doing terrible things to customers' food. If I hadn't been in the kitchen, I wouldn't have been able to prevent something bad from occurring one night.

A server had a table of Arabic men who were demanding and rude. Their waiter was fed up and decided that he was going to pour bacon fat on their meal. Arabs do not eat pork, and the waiter claimed that if they ate the tainted food, they wouldn't be allowed into heaven. Whether the men were jerks or not, I wouldn't permit that. I made sure to run the food.

IT'S TAKING FOREVER

On my second night of training, a family of four came in. I seated them and placed their order. The line cooks were chatting outside because they thought the restaurant was empty. They had no idea an order came in, and I didn't know that I was supposed to alert them.

73

Stephanie, the tall redhead, had neglected to tell me to check on orders. She stepped out for a break. I assumed she would take care of the order when she returned from her break. But ... she was in her car shooting up heroin. A while later, the furious mother at my very first table *ever* called me over. "Where's our food?"

I apologized and said I was new.

She responded, "Well, I'm gonna break you in. We've been waiting forever! This is ridiculous. It's late. I have *two* kids who have to be up *early* for school tomorrow. We ordered a burger and fajitas! What the *heck* is taking *so long?* This is insane. Get our food out here! Now!"

I'm pretty sure she wouldn't have been so selective about her wording had her kids not been there. When a customer treats a waiter like shit, it ruins the waiter's night. Subconsciously, the waiter might be rude to the rest of his customers, which results in lousy tips.

Some people are pissed off before they sit down. Poor or slow service has nothing to do with these diners' attitudes. One night, two friends came in for dinner. They flagged down Amanda, one of our most professional waiters.

"Hey, can we get a waiter or what?"

Amanda explained that she wasn't serving their section, but she would find Brad, their waiter. The man snapped, "Well, can we at least get some drinks?"

I HAVE A QUESTION

On a slow night, a waiter might find amusement in the fact that you have forty-one questions about a certain entree. On busy nights, don't hold your waiter hostage while you inquire where the chickens come from.

During my first week waiting tables, a guy asked me the most ridiculous questions about the menu. He was torn between two entrees, as though he'd never had a quesadilla or fajitas before. Finally, he asked me to make a recommendation and then yelled at me for making a "crappy decision."

At White Spice, I ran food to a table of inquisitive men who wanted to know how much the average halibut weighs. (Employees must precede all questions to the chef using the phrase, "Chef, please." This gives him a heads up so as to not distract him from his work.)

"Chef, please? The men at table thirteen want to know how much the average halibut weighs."

"Four hundred pounds."

When I returned to their table, they wanted to know what *their* particular halibut weighed.

"Chef, please? The men at table thirteen want to know how much their particular halibut weighed."

He rolled his eyes and then cracked a mischievous smile. Had the restaurant been busy, Chef would have told me to fuck off with the stupid questions, but he played along and said, "Tell these morons they're eating the largest halibut I've *ever* seen. Tell them it weighed six hundred fifty pounds."

The men were blown away and asked where the halibut had come from. I headed back to the kitchen, "Chef, please? The men at table thirteen want to know where the halibut came from."

"Who the fuck *are* these people? We get our halibut from Alaska. The fish was named Anthony. He had a wife, two kids, and a dog."

NO TIP FOR YOU

A couple came in for dinner and asked their waiter, Amanda, for the list of beers priced under happy hour specials. Amanda mistakenly included Corona, which they ordered. When their bill arrived, the Corona wasn't discounted. The guy hit the roof. (The Corona was seventy-five cents more than the happy hour beers.) Of course, Amanda apologized.

He told her to remove the beers from his check or he would not tip her. Amanda needed a manager's okay to remove the beer from the bill, but the diners were in a hurry. They left a tip … seventy-five cents on their forty-dollar meal.

People who threaten not to tip aren't aware or don't care that waiters' incomes are dependent on tips. If your food is cold or your martini isn't up to par, don't penalize your waiter. A guy orders a steak and requests medium well, cuts into it, and discovers it's rare. He loses his mind and insists his request was neglected. Give your waiter the benefit of the doubt. Her job isn't to cook your food or mix your drink. If your problem lies in an aspect besides service, complain to management.

After working at White Spice, I became aware of fine dining protocol. Initially I thought the emphasis on the placement of a dish was pretentious. However, it's all part of the show. If you know to look for it, you will expect it. Although I don't tip less when a food runner at a three- or four-star restaurant doesn't present the dish properly, I wonder why the proper serving technique wasn't taught.

If you do have a waiter who is rude or inattentive, feel free to show your dissatisfaction with a poor tip. Otherwise, 20 percent is standard in larger cities.

Sometimes, however, the percentage you tip is irrelevant. A 20 percent tip on a bagel and coffee in a diner is fifty cents.

If your total bill is less than five dollars, the percentage of your tip doesn't matter. Fifty cents ain't gonna pay the bills.

STEREOTYPES ABOUT CRAPPY TIPPERS

In my two years at the Texas Café, I worked with fifty waiters and more than thirteen managers. Almost every one of them had experience in other restaurants and brought their stereotypes with them.

If you are black, old, or foreign, you're a shitty tipper.

The *number one* stereotype I encountered was that African American people are shitty tippers.

A waiter had five tables. One table was occupied by black diners and four tables by white diners. The waiter got three poor tips, one from the black diners and two from the white diners. The justification for the poor tip from the white guys was, "He's a jerk." When a black family walked in, a waiter or two grumbled, "Okay, who wants the crappy tipper?"

An elderly man brought his family of twelve in for dinner. The total bill was $150. A twenty percent tip would be $30; he left $6. About an hour later, the man's grown son returned, found his waiter, apologized, and gave her $40.

In most European countries and in Australia, tipping is included in the cost of the meal. I guess waiters there love American tourists (on second thought, they probably *hate* American tourists) who leave extra money.

Most foreigners who came into the Texas Café either pretended not to understand the American tipping system or weren't aware. A typical tip on a forty-dollar meal from non-English speaking folks? Two dollars.

CAMPING OUT

Camping out is the most salary-debilitating thing a customer can do to his waiter. Even in a welcoming neighborhood restaurant, diners should be cognizant of this. If you came in at six and you last ordered a menu item at seven and now it's ten, your waiter is not making money.

In the three hours you camped at the table without ordering, the waiter could have had three or four additional seatings. If you're in for the long haul, let your waiter know and make it worth his while. Every hour is another tip that you've prevented him from earning. The average tip at the Texas Café was eight dollars, so in the three hours you sat chatting, that's about twenty-four dollars the waiter didn't earn.

If you're dead set on camping out, double the tip. But since no one does that, just leave early.

I HAVE A COUPON

I never realized that putting together the Top Rope Fitness/Texas Café promotion would piss off so many waiters. I thought it would be a great way to attract new customers. But it also attracted cheap idiots.

The waiters held a friendly grudge against me because customers would tip on the discounted price. I was amazed by how many people did this. If you have a coupon for a free or discounted meal, tip on the original price before the discount. Don't penalize your waiter.

KIDS

If you can afford to go out for dinner, you can afford a babysitter. Unless your child is the crown prince, keep his screaming, crying, disruptive ass at home (same goes for the movies).

An uncontrollable kid will ruin your dinner, but more important, your baby will ruin other diners' evening out. Parents need to keep an eye on antsy children. The worst kids are the ones who run from table to table clothes-lining the salt and pepper shakers to the floor. In restaurants that provide crayons and paper for the kids, the idea is to draw on the paper, not the *walls*.

Parents may think it's cute that their kid is expressing his artistic nature, but I bet you the busboy who has to scrub the crayon markings off the walls is thinking something else.

And what is the deal with Cheerios in plastic baggies? If your child is supposed to be *eating* them, why do 80 percent of these little round oats end up on the floor? I don't expect parents to clean the floors, but at least don't permit a mess like that. And tip more, because sweeping up crushed Cheerios isn't what your busboy should be doing.

Kids get bored, whine, scream, and cry. Tell your waiter to bring out your children's food first. Most kids take *forever* to eat. When your food arrives, they'll still be working on their meals. Quietly.

A young mother brought her hyperactive three-year-old in for lunch. Luckily, there was only one other couple in the dining room. Unfortunately for those two, their lunch was ruined. The three-year-old began to climb over all the booths and across the tables while screaming and ripping off her clothes.

Brad and I stood in disbelief, watching mom try to calm her psycho daughter to no avail. The girl ran table to table, threw sugar packets into the air, and pushed all the silverware to the floor. It was a bad day to be a fork.

CELL PHONES

Eight-two percent of Americans own cell phones. I would wager roughly the same percentage is offended by people who use them in restaurants. Gyms prohibit cell phone use. Movie theaters with talking popcorn remind you to turn off your phone.

Nothing sucks more than hearing only one side of what sounds like an interesting conversation.

STUPID CUSTOMERS

Stupid customers aren't necessarily rude people. They're just oblivious to their surroundings. From drunks to morons, customers who keep us entertained or frustrated are never in short supply.

One night when the Texas Café was filled to capacity, a man approached our largest table of diners with this request: "We want this table. Can you finish your meal now so we can have it?"

Amazingly, the diners requested that their food be wrapped up to go and they left. Had someone asked me to rush through my meal so he could have my table, I would have told the guy where he could sit.

DRUNKS

A group of middle-aged men were enjoying a quiet dinner together. Insert a group of twelve drunk college students, and you have a recipe for disaster. The students were plastered when they arrived. They ordered several more drinks. Within minutes, they were shouting and making inappropriate jokes in front of children.

Had I been the manager, I would have thrown them out. But that night's manager decided to keep a close eye on them. Their noise level increased. The manager was finally going to intervene when one of the middle-aged men turned to the rowdy college kids and said, "Hey! You all shut the fuck up! We're trying to enjoy our dinner over here!"

After his polite request, the college guys left.

ELBOWS SPEAK LOUDER THAN WORDS

Customers forget that waiters balance heavy trays on their shoulders. One evening, a customer slid out of his booth, a la Dukes of Hazard, and nearly collided with my tray of sizzling fajitas.

Another time, after a big meal, a diner decided to kick back in his chair. His action obstructed a walkway. We could have told him that he risked tripping a server, but where's the fun in that? Instead, we *accidentally* elbowed him in the head every time we walked by. He got the message.

I'D LIKE TO RETURN THIS

A woman who lived in my building frequented the Texas Café. I had been on the job a short while and already dreaded seeing her. She was notorious for causing a big scene. She had three entrees she ordered in rotation. After one bite, she demanded to see me. She complained and ordered a different entree. The Texas Café comped her meal.

The crab quesadilla never had enough crab. The taco/enchilada combo had too much rice and beans. The beef tacos had very little meat.

Devon, the floor manager, decided to put an end to her shenanigans. She ordered one of her three entree choices and promptly issued her standard complaint. I watched from the kitchen with the rest of the staff as Devon cut into her. "Every week, you order something and then send it back. You're rude and you cause a scene. You're costing the Texas Café money. Get out of my restaurant *now* and *never come back*. You are banned from this restaurant."

She shouted as he escorted her out of the restaurant. She was never seen again ... at least at the Texas Café. Several weeks later, I saw her in the lobby of my building. She asked, "Does that stupid black man still work there?"

He didn't, but I told her he did, and I told her not to refer to him that way.

I admired Devon because he wasn't afraid to break the corporate rules. Other managers would have called the corporate office to ask how to address this situation. Devon took matters into his own hands, and, in this case, it was the right thing to do. He put an end to her scam. The customer *isn't* always right.

IT ALL COMES FULL CIRCLE

On any given night, the wait staff at your local restaurant has its share of drunk, stupid, obnoxious, thoughtless, demanding, and rude customers. In high school, you learn to deal with nasty teachers. In college, you may have a roommate who sucks. In the work world, your boss may be a jerk. But in the restaurant world, you deal with the roommate, the boss, *and* the teacher you don't like. Your job depends on remaining calm, patient, and polite, no matter how much you may want to stick a fork in someone's eye.

Customers should assume equal responsibility for good behavior. If your waiter looks frazzled, don't give him a hard time. Although a waiter should have everything under control and maintain a poker face, some waiters have been reduced to tears by nasty customers.

If students are considering taking a year off before college, they should jump at the chance to work in a restaurant. One year dealing with rude customers is incredibly beneficial in the long run. Better to learn these people skills before embarking on your life's work.

Chapter Ten
It's A Miracle They Ain't Dead Yet

Ordering exact food quantities is a challenge when you can't predict how a restaurant will do on any given night. Leftovers are turned into the specials for the next night. For New Year's Eve, Carl decided to offer lobster tails and filet mignon. People didn't come to the Texas Café prepared to spend that kind of money. Advertising the special entrees in advance might have helped, but he didn't. Lobster tail was in abundance by the evening's end. How could we use these tails for tomorrow's menu? Lobster quesadillas? They sold like mad.

Seafood was not a big seller at the Texas Café, so spending big bucks on fresh seafood was a waste. Despite the fact that the seafood was shrink-wrapped, flash frozen, and shipped from a warehouse, we were told to tell customers it was fresh.

Big sellers like beef, chicken, dairy, eggs, and vegetables were always fresh. Cheese and jalapeños for the queso dip arrived in a can. So did the tomatoes for red rice. The tortilla chips were fried off premises, packed, boxed, shipped, and placed in dry storage. The Texas Café switched from fresh avocados for its guacamole to pre-mashed containers of avocados. Enchiladas were made in mass quantities and sat in the walk-in fridge for days. Spinach and feta enchiladas—the best tasting—were the least popular entrees, so they were only made once a week, on Sundays. By Friday, the tortillas were either dried out or covered in mold. Customers complained that the enchiladas were crunchy when they should be soft. We should have made smaller quantities more frequently since they didn't sell often. Instead, management suggested cooks cover the tortillas in more sauce to moisten them when they dried out.

All in all, Tex-Mex food is relatively easy to plan for, because all dishes are composed of virtually the same ingredients.

In comedian Jim Gaffigan's act *Doin' My Time*, he says, "I used to be a waiter in a Mexican restaurant in Indiana. That's where you wanna go for Mexican, Indiana or Belgium, you know? Mexican food is the best, but it is all the same. It's almost a conspiracy. It's like they had a meeting two hundred years ago in Mexico, and one guy stood up and said, 'Hey, look, the reason I got everyone here is pretty simple. I figured we could rename this one entree seven times, sell it to the Americans. The French said it was a good idea. Now, who's in on it?' One guy in the back stood up and said, 'Wouldn't that be dishonest?' 'Well, if you keep your mouth shut, we'll name one of the entrees after you. What's your name?' 'My name's Chimichanga.' That's a true story."

But, no matter how hard management tried to have everything on hand, we rarely did. Imagine running out of a staple of Mexican cooking like tortillas. I can't count the number of nights we ran out of tomatoes, avocados, sour cream, or even tortilla chips. No tomatoes meant no salsa. No avocados meant no guacamole.

A diner once said, "The Texas Café running out of tortillas is like the Olive Garden running out of spaghetti."

MY SPOON IS DIRTY AND THE DEATH OF LECHUGA MAN

A bucket of soapy water for dirty silverware sat on the dishwasher's line. Once the bucket was filled to the brim, the dishwasher stuck his hands in the murky, bacteria-ridden water and pulled out handfuls of filthy utensils. The utensils were placed on a plastic tray and run through the dishwasher. Then, without washing his hands, the dishwasher grabbed the now "clean" utensils and put them in separate containers for spoons, forks, and knives.

A dirty spoon might have been covered by another spoon. When you're sorting dozens of utensils every hour, dirty ones can be overlooked. So can a glass with a lipstick smudge on its rim. Always ask for a straw and say no lemon in your water, because who knows where your waiter's hands have been?

Ricardo, a dishwasher, was asked to prepare more shredded lettuce after we ran out. Do you really want a man who has been touching filthy dishes to go straight to cutting lettuce without washing his hands? Ricardo stood over a sink full of water to clean the lettuce he'd just chopped. He didn't take into consideration that his hands were dirty from washing dishes.

He continued to dunk his filthy hands into "clean" water that was intended to "clean" the "dirty" lettuce. The dirty lettuce was probably cleaner before he cleaned it. After the lettuce had been "cleaned," he stored it in a container and put it in the walk-in.

The water was now light brown. Suddenly, Ricardo cut his hand. He washed his bloody finger in that sink full of bacteria and dirt! At that moment, Manny wanted some vanilla ice cream. Instead of getting a spoon, he used his dirty fingernail to scoop out ice cream.

I made a habit of washing my hands every ten minutes and each time I touched raw food. I may have been the only line cook who routinely washed his hands.

I warned a friend not to eat at the Texas Café because the employees didn't wash their hands. She asked if there was a sign in the rest room. There sure was, but not all of the kitchen staff could read English, so the sign wasn't that useful.

IT'S STILL GOOD

Familiar with the five second rule? Welcome to many restaurants. The rule goes like this: If you drop an item of food on the floor, you have five seconds to pick it up before it becomes contaminated. The Texas Café had its own variation: It's still good no matter how long it's been on the floor.

That was the number-one problem I witnessed in the kitchen. Food—such as raw chicken—was dropped on the floor, picked up, and used. Imagine if the line cook stepped in dog shit on his way to work and dropped the chicken where he had been standing all night.

Most of the line cooks could not bring themselves to throw away food. Brushing or rinsing it off was good enough. When I saw food hit the floor, I insisted it be thrown away. I peeled potatoes over a trash can as part of the prep work. A potato slipped out of my hand and fell in the garbage. Another line cook pulled it out, wiped it off, and said, "It's okay. It's not dirty."

Rule of thumb: if it's in the trash can, it's dirty. Speaking of trash cans, Nelson, a dishwasher, sometimes did prep work when we were in a jam. He made the guacamole, which was very good, but he wedged a large plastic container in the trash can to mash the avocados. Allen joked, "Ahhh, nothin' like Nelson's Famous Trash Can Guacamole!"

The dinner shift ended, and the cooks were breaking down the line. Just as the rice was thrown away, a ticket came in for a large to-go order. The order called for one large container of rice. A cook took an empty water pitcher and scooped the trash-can rice into a to-go container.

Mid-scoop, Joan entered the kitchen. She was mortified. The cook explained that the order had just come in and the rice on top wasn't dirty.

Joan shouted, "The to-go order is for *me!*"

The embarrassed cook said, "Oh, I didn't know! I make fresh for you!"

Joan explained that it didn't matter *who* the rice was intended for. If it's in the garbage, it stays in the garbage. Between you and me ... I think it would have been okay to give Joan the trash-can rice.

ALLERGIES? LACTOSE INTOLERANT?

If you can't handle gluten or are lactose intolerant, a Tex-Mex restaurant probably isn't your best dining option. Many diners never alert their waiters to their allergies or special needs. A line cook who can barely speak English has no idea how to prepare your food if you're allergic to gluten.

If a menu isn't descriptive, tell your waiter ahead of time to hold whatever you don't like. Waiters aren't mind readers. But they should know the menu inside and out. When I trained new waiters on the expo line, I made sure they understood the importance of knowing every ingredient. The more you know, the more you make.

Imagine if a customer asked what was in the red rice and got a blank stare. Now imagine if the waiter could belt out every ingredient. Diners like to know they're being taken care of by a waiter who knows her stuff.

A diner was allergic to cilantro. His waiter came into the kitchen, got the menu description book, and attempted to memorize every dish that contained cilantro as though she were cramming for a test. The waiter might forget to mention the one entree that the guy would end up ordering. I told the customer myself. He was unable to order red rice, lime cilantro salad dressing, corn relish, shrimp tacos, beef (the marinade included cilantro), guacamole, pico de gallo, salsa, and enchiladas. In other words, go home.

A Middle Eastern man came in for dinner and sat at the bar. Leo, the bartender, was too busy to take his order. I helped out. The diner immediately informed me he could not eat pork. I punched in his order for beef fajitas and added "no pork."

Another server expedited the fajitas for my table. She was about to run the fajitas with a side of red beans. She saw the ticket that said "no pork" but didn't know or didn't register that red beans were made with bacon. I resolved the problem and told the diner why we substituted black beans. He was very impressed that I looked out for him.

DISEASES

Restaurant employees are among some of the most loyal employees in any field. They show up when they're sick, sometimes because they need the money but other times just to prove that nothing can hold them back from sweltering in a hot kitchen.

A line cook had pink eye. He didn't know how contagious it was, so he came into work preparing food with his hands while feverishly rubbing his eyes throughout the dinner rush. By the time a manager noticed, it was too late.

Working in the food industry while you're ill is wrong, but calling in sick is perceived as a sign of weakness. Endurance and a need to prove you have what it takes play a large role in your success.

Despite this willingness to prove you're tough, when a cook vomits in the trash can during prep work, a line must be drawn. Bragging rights are fine and dandy, but when the health of diners is in jeopardy, you have to put your "tough guy, nothing holds me back" ego down.

WATCH WHAT YOU EAT

My friend Cat worked in a highly regarded restaurant chain. She told me the following story. A man came into dinner with a party of twenty. The group was midway through dinner when one of the diners discovered a rusty nail in his food.

The weirdest thing a customer found in his food at the Texas Café was a rubber band. Amanda found a dead bumble bee in the shredded lettuce. I was preparing an order of guacamole when I spotted something in the container.

"Hey, what *is* that?"

Dan came over and took a look. He grabbed a spoon and poked at it. We leaned in for a closer look when, all of a sudden, it moved.

"Oh shit! Shit!"

We leapt back, shrieked like Jamie Lee Curtis in *Halloween*, and grabbed onto each other in horror as a moth flew out of the guacamole. Dan looked to me and said, "If anyone asks … it wasn't a moth, it was a flying rat. And there were ten of them."

I'M A VEGETARIAN

Not if you eat out you're not! The layout of the Texas Café kitchen was impractical for vegetarians. White Spice used separate frying pans for vegetarian orders, but if a major chain like the Texas Café didn't have a practical kitchen layout, I'd wager a lot of restaurant kitchens don't. A vat of queso (vegetarian friendly cheese dip) sat next to cooked beef waiting to be served. Sometimes, juices from the cooked steak found their way into the queso.

Ground beef and chicken stew (*pollo guisado*) were located behind the vegetarian-friendly sauces for burritos and enchiladas. When a line cook used a slotted spoon to drain the chicken broth, the broth dripped into the once vegetarian-friendly sauces. Rearranging the order of the meat and sauce would have resolved this problem. But the line cooks had their established habits, and no matter how often I tried to rearrange them, the cooks went back to their old ways.

Ryann used to make a quick bite to eat when we had down time after the dinner rush. Her dinner usually consisted of rice and beans, but one night, she opted for enchiladas. Three bites into her cheese enchiladas, she discovered she was eating chicken. Manny had accidentally grabbed chicken enchiladas. When she informed him she was a vegetarian, he shot her a confused look and insisted there were vegetables in the enchiladas.

I hope cooks do not screw over vegetarians on purpose. But accidents, poor layout, and non-English-speaking line cooks can create problems. A cook preparing a vegetable burrito using a frying pan that moments ago was used for cooking bacon was a common occurrence. Vegetarian? Your safest bet is a vegetarian restaurant.

THE WALK-IN

The walk-in fridge at the Texas Café was the cause of numerous problems. I learned a valuable rule from Meghan when I started working at the Texas Café.

Raw foods *had* to be stored on the bottom shelf but *never* on the floor (as this was a health code violation). If raw beef was placed above lettuce and a cook removed a piece of meat with tongs, blood and raw beef juice dripped onto the lettuce. Amazingly, this rule was always followed, but ultimately it didn't matter. Animal juice splatters were inevitable.

Health code violations took a back seat when Celia increased catering orders. The walk-in fridge became a storage unit for catering orders. Accessing foods required for the restaurant became increasingly difficult when large catering boxes took over the shelf space.

The kitchen was running out of room as catering expanded. Food was relocated in the walk-in fridge according to Celia's priorities. Condiments that didn't pertain to immediate catering orders were moved next to or below raw meats.

Maybe the walk-in fridge was filled beyond capacity or maybe it was just old, but during the beginning of our dinner rush, it broke down. A ten-pound block of ice formed around the freezer motor, preventing cool air from circulating. The temperature climbed from 37 to nearly 70 degrees.

With raw eggs, cheese, sour cream, milk, and meat in the fridge, we either had to cook quickly or throw away a lot of food. Richard worked with a chef's knife chipping away at the ice block in an attempt to save thousands of dollars worth of food. The temperature began to drop.

A new waiter decided to stack five cases of raw eggs on top of one another in the walk-in. Eggs typically went in the outside walk-in where there was more room.

I went into the walk-in to get some guacamole and saw a thousand raw eggs stacked hazardously on top of one another. I told the new guy to move the eggs to the proper place. Just as he opened the door, there was a collective "oh Jesus" as the bottom box of eggs buckled under the weight.

Five cases of raw eggs tumbled to the floor as we stood by helplessly.

SOUR CREAM

Allen returned to the Texas Café after completing his first year of culinary school and resumed waiting tables. But through school he had become interested in food safety. He asked me to help look for our thermometer to run some tests in our kitchen. The temperature of hot food must register 140 degrees or above. Cold foods such as sour cream and mayonnaise must be kept below 41 degrees to be considered safe.

We tested the sour cream and chipotle mayonnaise that sat on a bed of ice that was changed hourly. We were shocked when the sour cream clocked in at 80 degrees Fahrenheit. After the chipotle mayo hit 100 degrees, we had to collect our jaws from the floor.

We heard that the kitchen might be remodeled. New technology would eliminate the need for ice and would control the temperature of products than could spoil in high heat. The upgrades never happened.

Chapter Eleven
The End Is Near

Management had changed *again*. Both employees and loyal diners lost faith in the Texas Café. Celia never liked Carl and wanted him demoted. The corporate office had a lot of faith in Celia. They appointed her the new general manager and relocated Carl.

Celia was "running" the catering division, so she gave the duties of GM to Alex but retained the final say in every decision. Alex had aspired to the GM position for a long time. He didn't want to blow this opportunity, but he knew it would be tricky. He didn't approve of Celia's methods, but challenging her authority would get him fired. He did the best he could.

The Texas Café grew to ten locations, and the corporation ran four other highly successful restaurants in the city. But in less than two years, I witnessed the decline of the chain's most popular neighborhood restaurant. Typically, this business has no middle ground. It's sink or swim. But thanks to the financial backing of the corporate office, the Texas Café was in a perpetual sink. Celia's revamping of the catering division gave the appearance of greater success.

Sometimes the ups and downs in the business cannot be explained. One afternoon, the dining room was surprisingly packed. Four catering orders needed to go out. The kitchen was full of confused waiters asking for their orders. Frantic catering employees barked orders to the line cooks.

Since the cooks were told to hustle the catering orders and Celia didn't give a shit about the diners, I took charge and went behind the line to cook. We didn't want angry diners. They tip less. Lesser tips result in the exodus of waiters. When capable waiters quit, the restaurant's staff has to hire new waiters, train them, and deal with their initial mistakes. For every good employee who exits, numerous replacements do not work out.

I cooked in a crammed kitchen, getting the food out as fast as possible. I apologized to diners on behalf of the kitchen. Customers got their food, waiters got their tips, and no one quit (that day). But the Texas Café was sinking faster than my interest in coming up with a witty analogy. I realized I wanted out.

SINKING SHIP

Despite the painfully obvious trend in management's focus toward catering, people were still vying for promotions. Why jump onto a sinking ship? The neighborhood had turned its back on us. Locals no longer wanted to support a restaurant where employees were fired and hired quicker than a hiccup. Our loyal diners stopped coming.

The restaurant would have closed if catering hadn't provided income. Celia decided to cut costs. She fired the window washer and gave that responsibility to the waiters. Karmah was looking for a reason to quit. Washing windows was as good as any.

"If the restaurant is empty, I'm not earning money. If they want me to clean, they can pay me."

Our five best waiters quit. Alex was a nervous wreck. He was desperate for waiters and hired whoever walked in. But who would train them? Arielle, a new manager who was hired by her friend, Celia, had no idea what she was doing. Celia made sporadic appearances in the dining room and announced changes that were disasters waiting to happen.

Celia fired Nelson because he was paid too much. In her eyes, paying an efficient dishwasher what he had earned in raises over *many* years was a waste of money. I felt paying more money for hardworking, loyal employees made more sense.

Management was losing control of the business. These cost-cutting decisions cost more money, time, and unnecessary headaches. Celia's friends were offered catering positions, which paid big bucks, while loyal and deserving waiters were not. Amanda would have jumped at this opportunity.

In 2003, Meghan ran the Texas Café with ease. She knew her employees had a strong work ethic. They had pride in their work and a vested interest in the success of the restaurant. Amy, a waiter, came to work with a broken leg. Not only did she wait on tables, but she insisted on carrying her own trays! The waiters wanted to earn as much money as possible, so they took the time to learn about the menu and the many ingredients in each dish. They could handle stress. The restaurant operated with two waiters downstairs and one waiter upstairs. Fewer waiters meant more money.

In 2004, the corporate office noticed that sales were down. Its explanation? Crappy service. More waiters were required to remedy the nonexistent problem. Had managers in the corporate office brought their asses into the Texas Café on a Friday night, they would see why sales were down. The restaurant was empty! But Celia did what was necessary to keep her job.

Amanda was stuck upstairs on a slow night, and now a new waiter joined her.

"It's all fine and dandy that they're experimenting, but this is my income, and I can't continue to lose money while they figure out what works," she told me.

She quit. Had Celia listened to Alex, our five best waiters wouldn't have quit. Why wasn't the corporate office concerned that five experienced waiters quit soon after Celia's promotion?

THE NEW GUYS

As the demands for catering increased, Carl's promise to hire a catering staff was finally realized eight months after he made it. Alex brought in ten new employees to assist with catering.

Once again, time was money, and no time would be spent on training. You would think that, with two thousand dollars on the line for each catering order, Celia would want the new staff fully trained. But she let them fend for themselves.

One morning I was in the kitchen setting up the expo line when Andrew, a new guy, walked in. He approached me and barked, "Hey! You're in my way! *Move!*"

First of all, I had no idea who this guy was. Second, Tim put the KENNY ZONE sticker up for a reason. I pointed to the sign and said,

"Actually, this is my station—so, technically, you're in *my* way. So *you* move."

That morning, four *huge* catering orders were in the works and four new employees were to deliver them. Renay decided she wanted extra income and asked if she could oversee the operation. She came in early to pack and label. All four orders were to go out at 3 PM, which she marked on each box. Each delivery guy received a print-out of the order and the customer's address.

As each catering guy arrived, he saw a box labeled 3 PM and assumed it was his delivery. I think you can surmise that each party received the wrong order.

Everyone was at fault. Renay should have put the customer's name on each box. The delivery crew should have double checked their orders, not only to be sure that the correct order was going to the correct party but to ensure that everything for the order was packed. Ultimately, Celia was at fault for not overseeing her own operation.

The following week, Andrew was in charge of a catering order valued at $2,200. He was visibly nervous. Andrew was talking to Ray, a new guy who had some previous experience in catering. He said, "Ray, I need all of the ingredients for the margarita mix."

Andrew wrote down the ingredients as Ray dictated: "Two gallons of water, one gallon of lime mix …"

Andrew loaded up his order and left. Moments later, Arielle, the manager, asked where the van was. Andrew had mistakenly taken the van! Now we had to find transportation for an order that was five times larger than Andrew's.

Meanwhile, Andrew left in such a tizzy that he forgot the tortillas, beef, and shrimp! He rushed back, got the beef and shrimp, but forgot the tortillas *again*. At the party, he prepared the margaritas but forgot to add water.

The host of the party called Arielle to complain. When Andrew returned, Arielle shouted at him for leaving the tortillas behind and omitting the water in the margarita mix. Andrew defended himself by saying, "I asked Ray for the ingredients. He never mentioned water!"

Luckily, I happened to be standing there. (Okay, not luckily—I knew he was coming back, and I wanted to see him get yelled at.) I piped in when he tried to blame Ray. "What? Are you *kidding?* I was standing right there when you asked him. You *wrote it down!* Don't pin your stupidity on Ray!"

He denied it, but Arielle wasn't *that* stupid. After all, Andrew had forgotten the beef, shrimp, and tortillas. When Celia fired him, he snapped and screamed, "Do you know who I am? I am the best employee you have! You can't fire me!"

TRAINING MY REPLACEMENT?

I walked in one morning to find a guy standing at the expo line, staring into space. He was the new expediter, hired to work the morning shifts, a time of day when expediting was unnecessary. He asked me when the expo would arrive.

After two weeks of training, the *only* thing he had learned was that tacos, burritos, and enchiladas were garnished with lettuce. He piled on so much lettuce, it was comical. He knew he was doing something right and joyfully shouted, "Oh! Oh! It gets lettuce! It gets lettuce!"

He made the same mistakes day in and day out and wasn't getting the hang of *anything*. No matter how many times I warned him that the plates coming out of the oven were extremely hot, he repeatedly grabbed them and shouted in pain.

REPERCUSSIONS ARE A BITCH

A woman came in with a party of twelve. She ordered green rice (white rice mixed with pureed tomatillo, not a spicy dish) for her kids, an option on the children's menu. She took one bite of the green rice, then screamed at Kerrie, "How *dare* you serve this to *children!* This is so spicy, it's *deadly!*"

Kerrie offered to replace the green rice. The woman rudely waved her off and ate the entire plate of rice. The rest of the meal went by without issue, and Kerrie provided good service.

An 18 percent gratuity was added to the bill, as was the policy with large parties. The woman took issue with the tip because the rice was spicy and Kerrie hadn't warned her. She demanded that Arielle remove the gratuity from the check. Arielle *should* have said, "I'm sorry, but you were offered a substitute that you declined and you ate the rice."

Arielle removed the gratuity. Kerrie received *no* tip, and she was fired two weeks later. Arielle claimed that the woman called the corporate office to complain about the poor service and spicy rice.

Kerrie didn't buy that. Although we had no proof, we think Arielle hadn't properly removed the gratuity from the credit card bill. The woman probably called the corporate office to complain after she received her bill.

Instead of taking responsibility, Arielle blamed Kerrie. A few days later, Arielle bragged about the incident, saying, "Oooh! It was fun firing Kerrie!"

Now *that's* quality management.

Corporations sometimes lose control of hiring practices when they grow too large. As a result, people with poor common sense and no integrity obtain positions of responsibility and negatively affect others' lives.

GOODBYE TO OCTAVIO

The guys in the kitchen liked to joke about people getting fired. They thought seeing my stunned reaction was a riot. Every week was Gomar's last. So when someone really *was* fired, I wasn't sure. When I was told Octavio had been fired, I played along because after eight years of employment, Octavio was one of our most valuable employees.

Octavio knew management was taking advantage of him, but he was afraid of being fired. I encouraged him to voice his complaints. Had he complained to *any* of the past managers, Joan included, they would have listened. He found the courage to complain to Celia about the negative impact of catering and about his inadequate salary.

"Well, if you don't like it, you're fired."

When the word got out to the few remaining long-time employees, who all admired Octavio, management said he had threatened a delivery man with a knife. Octavio had listened to my advice, and he got the ax. I felt guilty.

It is unfortunate that of all the managers he could have spoken to during his Texas Café career, he got the irrational one who made a snap decision to fire a loyal employee, a friendly colleague, and passionate cook.

BROKEN A/C

August 2003: Two months *before* I began working at the Texas Café, the air conditioning in the kitchen had not worked for two years. Meghan, in her first month as GM, opted to save money by waiting for fall weather. The heat would break, and the kitchen temp would be tolerable. A year later, as summer approached, the cooks warned me that the kitchen was about to get uncomfortably hot.

August 2004: The hotter the kitchen got, the more unbearable work became. Joan told us that the corporate office would not approve the twenty-thousand-dollar repair bill. If the dining room was without air conditioning, the A/C would be fixed ASAP. But in the kitchen, where customers weren't affected, who cared?

Experienced managers (or owners) know food spoils in a hot kitchen. (Remember chipotle mayonnaise at 100 degrees?) Bugs visit a hot kitchen, employees sweat buckets (over *your* food!) in a hot kitchen, and heat adversely affects everyone's work. By the end of 2004, Joan was gone. Megan, a waiter, asked Carl, the GM, to get the air conditioning fixed.

"Yeah, the cheese is melting in this heat. We can't serve this to a customer. We'll have to fix it."

In a kitchen where the average temperature rose to 120 degrees, cheese should be the last of your worries. What if an employee had heat stroke? A hardened kitchen vet might say, "You're a cook, damnit, you're not supposed to be comfortable!"

Stepping into the Texas Café kitchen, you had five seconds before sweat stained your shirt. If appearance is essential, customers must have been aghast at seeing sweat-drenched servers.

Before Carl could keep the cheese from melting, he was gone. But he knew that food-safety issues were a way to get results.

Alex knew the corporate office would listen to him when it came to customer safety. I noticed the prep guy peeling and de-veining shrimp and placing them in a bucket to be transferred to the fridge. Suddenly, the raw gray shrimp turned pink, cooked by the kitchen's heat! I told Alex, and he got the okay to fix the air conditioning. When he mentioned Joan's cost estimate of twenty thousand dollars, the repairman laughed and said, "Try more like three grand."

Had Joan placed a call a year ago, the air conditioning would have been fixed. Employees and food roasted in a kitchen for three summers because no one cared.

IMPERSONAL SURVEYS

A fine dining restaurant such as White Spice might have a forty-five-minute pre-shift meeting. Since the specials are more complex than "three-cheese quesadilla," servers need time to memorize the ingredients. The chef has the cooks practice the nightly specials. The servers sample these dishes to recommend them to diners.

Every night before the dinner rush, Meghan gathered the entire Texas Café staff for a ten-minute pre-shift meeting. We discussed menu specials and joked around. Meghan wrapped up by asking if we needed anything or had any questions. She fixed whatever problem was identified.

These were not cliché-driven pump-up-the-staff meetings full of corporate BS *energy and fun!* Meghan didn't motivate her staff through phony encouragement. She knew we were capable. Even Joan ran succinct pre-shift meetings.

Celia ended pre-shift meetings. She had the manager hand out a post-shift questionnaire that showed how little regard she had for her staff. Among the questions: How was your shift? What was the high and low point of your shift? If you could do something differently regarding tonight's shift, what would it be?

MY BREAKING POINT

Employing a part-time host for our busy weekend nights made sense. Deena, our fun-loving, ditzy host, arrived at 5 PM. She cleaned the menus, filled the mint jar, and made sure there were enough crayons and paper menus. At 9 PM she cleaned the menus again and clocked out.

After Deena quit, we operated a year and a half without a host. Any employee could seat customers in our small restaurant. When Celia arrived, we were inundated with hosts, including a host during weekdays for the one-hour lunch rush. One minute Celia was trying to conserve money by making waiters wash windows; the next, she was wasting money on hosts (who happened to be her friends). These new hosts arrived at 3 PM and stayed until closing. The hosts' set-up work took twenty minutes. I didn't have the luxury of three paid hours to set up my expo line. It took an hour to set up, which I did while orders came in.

Celia spent forty thousand dollars a year on hosts we didn't need.

Sasha, Celia's friend, told me she was making the transition from waiting tables to hosting because, "That's where the big bucks are."

What big bucks? Recalling Deena's hourly wage of $8.50, I was knocked backward. I asked her to repeat the sum.

"Twelve dollars an hour."

That couldn't be right, I thought. It had to be a mistake. I worked hard for $9.50, and management was throwing $12 at hosts? Sasha realized she shouldn't have revealed this and suggested I ask for a raise. Oh, really?

Two weeks later, I did just that. I asked to go from $9.50 to $11 per hour. Alex agreed that I deserved a raise and said he would talk to Celia.

Allen, a waiter, was outraged when I told him what the hosts were paid. "We don't need a host. Never have. They could fire the hosts, divide the twelve dollars among the kitchen staff, and make you guys happy."

The fact that Sasha, Monica, and Michelle were paid $12 because of who they knew while I remained at $9.50 was my breaking point. Sasha assured me Celia would give me what I asked for because she was a great manager. "The Texas Café would be foolish to lose you. No one would want your job! It's too demanding."

Based on the recent trend of firing valuable employees to replace them with Celia's less capable friends, the cards weren't in my favor.

Our managers rarely thought through the repercussions of their actions. "Think before you act" sounds trite, but I never realized how few people observe this motto.

I asked Richard for advice.

"Yeah, I believe they're being paid twelve bucks an hour. I'm sorry about that. It's a real injustice to you, but there is nothing I can do about it."

He advised me not to threaten to quit because Celia would fire me. I sought Alex's advice, too. After all, he was the acting GM. He laughed when I told him Sasha was being paid $12 an hour. He didn't believe it, so I asked Celia. She responded, "I don't know. I don't pay them. Arielle is in control of the salaries. Ask her."

Arielle said, "I hope they're not getting twelve! I'm in charge of payroll, and I wouldn't give them twelve!"

Alex came to me a day later with a proposal from Celia regarding my request for $11 an hour.

Celia suggested I work Thursdays and Fridays from 12 to 8 PM with a one-hour break before the dinner rush. The catch? The line cooks would come in at 6 instead of 4. From 12 to 4, I would expedite. At 4, I would jump to the line and cook, expedite, and do *all* the prep work for the night. Why? The line cooks got paid $18 an hour. Instead of paying two cooks $72 for two hours of work, she was hoping to spend $22 on *one* guy who would do three jobs.

1. Celia never planned to ask the cooks if they would accept a schedule change that would cost them $32 a night, two nights a week, a loss of $3,328 a year.

2. There is no chaos (which I would miss) from 12 to 7 or 3 to 6, when the restaurant is empty. I'd be chopping onions. *Boring.*

3. I'd be doing a *shit load* of work for very little money.

4. Sending me home on Thursday and Friday night at 8 PM, our busiest time? Just plain stupid.

Kerrie came in to collect her last paycheck. She offered me this advice: "Celia is seeing how much she can take advantage of you. Tell her, 'I don't accept this. I want my current schedule and the raise I requested. If you can't give that to me, I guess I'm going to have to give you notice.'"

This was a risk, but Kerrie hoped Celia would give me the raise. I knew that wasn't gonna happen and finally decided I was okay with leaving. I considered the pros and cons:

CONS

Under-appreciated.

Underpaid.

Management took advantage of their employees.

Celia showed favoritism toward her friends while ignoring veteran employees.

Regulars had stopped coming, and the congenial neighborhood hangout no longer existed.

A successful restaurant was crashing because of poor management.

PROS

Coworkers.
Comfortable in my expediting position.
Enjoyed the responsibility that came with my job.

There were not many reasons to stay.

Chapter Twelve

I Quit

Logically, the next step in my Texas Café career would have been a promotion to management, but I knew I would be miserable in a management position with this corporation.

Richard and Alex wanted to do so much for the place but were never given the chance. Richard felt terrible when Octavio was fired but had no say in that decision. Why would I want to work for a place where managers had no say? I was already frustrated in my position as an expediter. Corporate management wanted yes-men, not people who had legitimate concerns and creative initiatives.

Initially, my journal was composed of what I had learned, whom I had met, funny stories, and insights into business. As time progressed, my entries became frustrated, complaint-laden, and increasingly angry. When I reread them, I thought, *Jeez, this needs to be toned down!*

Despite all the bullshit, I loved working at Texas Café. Each night I was sure I wanted to quit, until I arrived at work.

One night, I walked Monica, a new host, to her car. Out of the blue, she said she couldn't believe she was getting twelve dollars an hour to host. That was the push I needed.

The next morning I headed inside and found Celia in the upstairs dining room. She was painting over the cartoon characters of cowboys, cacti, and scorpions—too childish, she thought. With her back to me, I asked if I could talk with her.

"Sure, what's up?"

I informed her that today would be my last day. She asked why. Still facing her back, I said, "I was lied to about the hosts' salaries. I discovered they are being paid more than me, and I feel taken advantage of. I'm disappointed. I don't work for liars. If you want, I'll work this shift, but today is my last day."

Still with her back to me, Celia said, "Okay, bye."

Celia never made eye contact with me. That's poor manners. Everybody has a price, but *nothing* could have kept me there.

I WAS CUT

I went into the kitchen and told my colleagues that it was my last day. I jumped right into work, acting as though I hadn't quit. After all, I had a kitchen to oversee one last time. An hour and half later, one of Celia's stooges came into the kitchen and told me I was cut.

I did my side work as usual. I cleaned and restocked the line, refilled the mayo, tomato chipotle, and sour cream squeeze bottles and iced the line as though I were coming back the next day. Saying goodbye to Max and Melvin, two cooks with whom I had grown close, was difficult.

I shook Max's hand; he gave me a hug. Melvin, who forced me to dance with him to Spanish music during many evenings while everyone laughed, hugged me.

I looked at a recent scar on my hand from a kitchen burn. Someone had left a frying pan handle over an open flame and turned the flame off just as I arrived. I grabbed the handle and yanked my hand back observing the red flesh that resembled melted string cheese. I worked the rest of the shift in agony.

The KENNY ZONE sticker that had been proudly displayed was a sad reminder of better days. I looked at Lettuce Guy and thought, "This is my replacement? Damn, they're fucked."

I think quitting a job you've loved might be similar to selling your first home. As a new homeowner, you cherish your home. There are good and bad memories and tons of stories. As the years go on, you decide for one reason or another that it is time to sell the home. As you're walking out, you see the new homeowner walk in with his contractor and say, "We're gonna *gut* this place."

Knowing full well that you no longer own the home but are still emotionally invested, you say, "No, you can't do that to my house!"

As I stood outside the Texas Café, I was amazed by how much had changed in two years. The exterior remained the same, but the heart of the restaurant had changed. And so had I. I'd become more knowledgeable about the working world. I had developed an awareness and appreciation for hard working, ethical people who contribute to the success of an operation.

MY RESIGNATION LETTER

I wrote a letter to the owner. I was still fighting for that place, hoping that it could become the Texas Café of 2003.

To the Owners:

I want to share my thoughts about my two-year experience at the Texas Café. The Texas Café is a neighborhood restaurant that has added to the goodwill of our community life. I have felt a great loyalty to the restaurant, knowing many of the families who frequent the Café and having the privilege to work alongside the hard working kitchen and wait staff.

I've loved my expo job, especially on busy nights and Sunday brunch, when the demand for organization and speed is urgent. In addition to my expo work, I've cooked, run food, taken orders from customers when waiters were busy, and assisted in numerous other capacities. Being named Employee of the Year was very gratifying.

I have worked for more than thirteen Texas Café managers during twenty-two months here! I tried to relate and respond to each one's unique style and new demands. I contributed marketing ideas to attract more customers, created ads, and negotiated a successful deal between Top Rope Fitness and Texas Café.

I expressed, in a respectful way, my discouragement about my salary after learning that two new part-time hosts were paid a higher hourly wage. I asked for an increase. I was offered an increase (still less than the new employees) with the caveat that I accept new hours at a less busy time of the day. This was a way for management to save money on cooks' wages by using me to cook for much lower hourly wages.

I find that I cannot accept this. It seems that I have far more invested in the success of this restaurant than many of the managers for whom I've worked. I can't help but wonder why the owners aren't more personally invested in the internal success of its restaurant.

Sincerely,
Kenneth L. Suna

As expected, I received no response.

THE FOLLOW-UP

I thought I would visit the Texas Café in a month or two to check out the scene. But my curiosity got the better of me two days after I had quit! I planned to stop in after working out at the gym, but I never got the chance.

I ran into Scott, one of the new catering guys. He told me Celia had approached him and asked if he would be interested in my position. He declined. The managers were scrambling to find someone. Lettuce Guy wasn't working out.

Two weeks later, I stopped in to pick up my last paycheck. Yet another new manager was already making an impression on the employees. A bad one.

I went upstairs to the office and was greeted by Celia, who turned her back to me again and said, "Your check is in the folder."

On my way out, I said hello to the kitchen guys. Lettuce Guy grabbed me by the shoulders and shouted, "You can't quit! Please! I'm *terrified!* I don't know what I'm doing! I'm so nervous when we get busy! Don't leave me hanging, man! Please!"

I ran into Monica on my walk home. What she said really surprised me.

"You know, Sasha and Michelle went to Celia and said, 'Please dock our pay and give the difference to Kenneth. Please don't let him go. We need him.'"

I was blown away by their generosity.

Chapter Thirteen

White Spice

I was hired on the spot to work as a food runner at White Spice, a high-end seafood restaurant. The GM told me that the Texas Café wasn't a *real* restaurant and that I'd be in for a rude awakening.

Peter, the food runner who trained me said, "I'll be impressed if you last the week."

New employees are treated to a barrage of insulting lectures full of anger and intimidation. This was the staff's way of weeding out the weak.

"Can you count, or are you a moron?"

"*This* is my left hand, and *this* is my right. Can you remember that?"

Peter was impressed when I didn't run out crying like the last food runner. I needed the job. Staying in a place I already hated was easier than continuing the job hunt. As my first week came to a close, Peter expressed relief that I was staying. He was tired of training a new person each week.

I voluntarily left nine months later. During that time, I was belittled, insulted, called a retard, and accused of calling the chef de cuisine a liar. If the GM made a joke and you laughed, he told you to shut the fuck up. I discovered my passion for the restaurant business at the Texas Café; it died at White Spice.

The general manager towered over his staff at six-foot-five. He tipped the scales at close to three hundred pounds, but don't get the wrong impression. He was far from overweight. His muscles had muscles. By the end of each night, he rolled up his sleeves to reveal tattoos of barbed wire and skulls wrapped around his twenty-four inch pythons. The words ANGER and FEAR were interwoven through the tattoos. With his long black hair tied in a ponytail and a Captain Blackbeard beard, he was an imposing guy. When asked about the tattoos, he explained that his life was a constant circle of anger and fear.

"My angers fuel my fears, and my fears fuel my angers. RAGE is tattooed on my chest, away from me, and HOPE on my back, always nearby."

He shared this story: In a smoky bar, a woman noticed writing on the GM's forearms. She saw part of the tattoo.

"Does your tattoo say angel bear?"

He showed her his tattoos and responded, "Do I look like an angel bear to you, bitch?"

He opened up to me in a way I didn't anticipate by explaining his management style. He was not a bully for the fun of it. If he yelled at someone, it was because she fucked up. He knew she was capable of doing a better job. I asked if he thought a more toned-down approach would work; he dismissed that idea. He ruled by intimidation. "I yell because you fear it. And if you fear something, you will do everything in your *power* to make sure it *never* happens again."

Because employees dwelled on these dreadful lectures, fuck ups were unavoidable. Morale was poor. The stress affected each of us differently. If you were unable to adapt to it, you quit or got fired. Management wanted to get in your head and make you question your abilities. The GM might ask who ran the food to a certain table. I fessed up, assuming I had done something wrong. I learned not to second guess myself.

My job was threatened by the GM eight times. It became a running joke that every night was my last.

I DON'T LIKE YOUR STYLE

The night we spoke about his tattoos seemed an appropriate time to tell the GM that I didn't like being yelled at. Standing up to a person can create respect, or it can get you fired. Luckily, the GM was impressed that I had the balls to stand up to him. He told me not to take his yelling personally.

He would not have revealed his style if he didn't respect me. Suddenly, the lectures stopped. No hello when I walked in and rarely a goodbye when I left. By not speaking to me, he was letting me know I was doing okay.

But that didn't mean I was off the hook. I still had to deal with the chef de cuisine. Chef was your typical plate-throwing, hissy-fit, temper-tantrum prima donna. Professionals should be able to remain calm under the most brutal circumstances. Chef tried to motivate his cooks through threats.

"One more mistake and you all come in at six tomorrow morning to clean the kitchen from floor to ceiling."

Or:

"One more mistake and you step off the line and go home, and we all suffer as a result of your incompetence."

Working with the executive sous chef, Elliot, and the sous chef, Diandra, was easier. If a customer complained, they resolved the issue without throwing food in the trash or cursing. Elliot opened the sliding-glass doors that separated the kitchen from the dining room. He was proud of his job and wanted to show off. He was in control and confident. Stress didn't scare him.

Had our restaurant been a reality TV show, Elliot would get no ratings. Chef, like Gordon Ramsey on the hit TV show *Hell's Kitchen*, would get ratings for his over-the-top cursing and screaming.

Chef never allowed me to pour the *baniyuls* sauce for the oysters, sniff to check for bad ones, or stamp the ticket and run the food myself. It was his kitchen, damnit, and I had better not start doing his job.

If Elliot was busy with another order and oysters came up, I told him they were ready. If I tried that with Chef, he'd bark back that I was not in charge of the kitchen and to keep my mouth shut. But Elliot calmly told me to sell the oysters.

I admired Elliot's confidence. Diandra and Elliot patted you on the back and lit a fire under your ass at the same time. They empowered you to do your job better and faster. Chef, on the other hand, just put his foot up your ass.

On the expo table, where Chef put plates in order of table positions, were about twenty glass underliner plates used for soups and mussels. We quickly ran out on busy nights, but Chef didn't care. He would shout at the top of his lungs that I had *better* go to the dish-room and "not fucking *dare* return without underliners." If they were all in use, I was unable magically to produce plates. He suggested I wait until they were washed. If I waited, I was yelled at for not running food. Why not order more plates?

I had learned how to read people at the Texas Café and applied this by judging when it was appropriate to ask questions. I asked the GM questions … after he had a few rum and cokes.

Since Chef never ran food, he didn't realize how much room two huge designer plates took up on a table for two. People ordered numerous appetizers; arranging the table for these plates was challenging. Diners were not interested in watching me play Tetris. Tuna Tian, a raw tuna appetizer, was served on an oversized plate. When I suggested putting it on a smaller plate, Chef said I wasn't paid to think. But if I rephrased my statement as a question and asked if *he* thought we should use smaller plates, this gave him the power to decide. A few weeks later, when Chef ran food to his family, he realized that the plates were too big. Smaller plates were used from then on.

HARD WORKERS

Chef called for a runner when it was time to sell the food. At a table of four, each guest's position was labeled from one to four; the food was coordinated accordingly. "Snapper one, Big Eye two, Butt [halibut] three, Softie [soft shell crab] four." White Spice's motto was "two hands, two plates." The odd-numbered plate went in your left hand, even-numbered plate in your right. Each runner repeated what he was taking so Chef knew who was responsible for which dish and that the order was pronounced correctly.

Women were served first, unless seated at a booth, in which case the farthest diner in the booth was served first to avoid reaching over already placed food. All food was served palm up facing the guest. The back of the hand was considered a sign of disrespect.

According to the GM and Chef, running food was the most important aspect of the restaurant business. Wouldn't cooks be the most important players? After all, without them, we'd just be a room with tables and chairs.

Chefs and cooks are among the hardest-working people. They stand behind a grill for fifteen hours. Jermaine, one of the line cooks, got a phone call on Mother's Day. His grandmother had suffered a heart attack and was in serious condition. But he worked the rest of his shift. Surely, every cook would have understood if he had left, but Jermaine would be inconveniencing them, and so he stayed. Chef took it easy on Jermaine.

Chefs and cooks must have an incredible memory. Orders are called out in the order they come in. Cooks *must* communicate with one another. Each White Spice cook has his or her own station on the line: salads/apps, grill, broiler and deep fryer, oven and sauté. One entree might take five minutes to prepare; another takes twenty. The twenty-minute entree guy must tell the five-minute guy when his dish has five minutes left so the five-minute guy can start cooking his dish. Timing is precious in a restaurant's kitchen, but Chef always had time to rip a cook to shit if he screwed something up.

If broiler guy's scallops were in the window on time and sauté station guy was running late with the snapper, Chef tossed the scallops in the trash and told the sauté station guy he was a fuck up. The broiler guy had to prepare a new order of scallops.

Why do some chefs have a nasty reputation? They're in before 9 AM creating and preparing the menu and ordering food from the purveyors. By 5 PM, their night is *just* getting started. At 10 PM, chefs are tired of being on their feet all day. It's easy to see why the slightest mistake or complaint sends them over the edge. Winning an award makes the working environment even more challenging. If the food is good, chefs must live up to the hype and the diners' expectations.

If chefs are such jerks, why do people continue to work for them? Loyalty or convenience? The professional servers at White Spice were among the best. They remained at White Spice even though they could get a serving job anywhere. I doubt loyalty played a part in their decisions to stay. The restaurant was very successful, which meant steady income. They knew the menu and knew what to expect. And diners often requested the same server when they placed a reservation.

Servers tasted the specials of the night during pre-shift. The GM quizzed them.

"Which wines should they pair with the specials?"

A server responded, "The bright fruits in the pinot noir will go perfectly with the lamb special."

The GM nodded approvingly, "That's bullshit ... but it's good bullshit, and they'll buy the wine."

Every server frantically jotted down the script.

DOUBLE STANDARDS AND KISS UPS

Some employees were excused from certain kitchen duties or rules. Jake, the chef's buddy, kept his job despite his refusal to work his share. He showed up too late to do his opening side work. He ran some food and then stood around the remainder of the evening while other food runners did his closing side work. He was never reprimanded.

Peter said, "He doesn't work here when he works here."

Two trays of coffee came up in the barista station window. I asked Jake for a hand. He smirked and said, "I don't wanna." I thought he was joking until he walked away. Later that night he asked me for a ride home. I smirked and said, "I don't wanna."

The GM expected everyone to work as hard as he did. He tried numerous times to fire Jake, but Chef prevented it. On Sunday nights, when we were typically slow, Jake was paid to arrive an hour before me to do the opening side work. When I arrived minutes before opening, I asked him if he had completed his work. His response was always the same: "Nope." I had the GM change my arrival time to one hour earlier so I wouldn't have to scramble to complete the setup while Jake sat chatting.

I did learn a lesson in discretion thanks to Jake. Initially unaware of his friendship with Chef, I complained that I thought Chef was impossible to work for. Whoops. Jake told Chef. The longer I worked at White Spice, though, the more I doubted Jake's claim of friendship with Chef. I think Chef kept him around because Jake gave him constant praise.

Certain hosts received a meal at the end of the night. Food runners and servers who busted their asses got nothing. After especially brutal nights, Chef would buy the line cooks a drink. When Jake worked as a barista, he was offered a drink. When Peter worked as a barista, what do you think he was offered?

Thirty-two ounces of bottled water sold for twelve dollars at White Spice. A party of five ordered seven bottles throughout their meal. Their Turkish server overheard them complaining about high gas prices and stormed into the kitchen.

"Look at those motherfuckers at fifty-two. Do you believe these fucking idiots? They complain about the price of gas, but you see? They spend eighty-four dollars on *water!!*"

How 'bout a Shave?

Appearance was critical. We had to look professional: hair combed, no beard unless groomed, shirts tucked in, pants pressed, and shoes polished.

I wasn't a fan of these rules. The Texas Café's lax rules had spoiled me. However, I soon grew to respect White Spice's rationale for implementing these rules. Except for shaving daily. What a pain in the ass. The GM said, "The next time you come into work with stubble on your face, you will go to the Safeway, buy a razor, come back, and you will shave your face in the men's room. Are we clear?"

In The Blink of an Eye

Some people in this business are very private. Disappearing, never to be seen again, is how a lot of these folks roll. Peter told me he was contemplating leaving. I arrived at work the next night to find the GM smoking a cigarette while anxiously pacing in the parking lot. He took one look at me and said,

"Did you iron your pants?"

"Yes ... no."

"Look, Peter moved home to North Carolina this morning. You're the head food runner now. That means no more fucking up, okay?"

Before I could respond, he threw his cigarette on the ground, stomped on it, and went back inside.

Five months after I left, I noticed a White Spice ad seeking a general manager. I e-mailed some White Spice guys to get the low-down, but they had no idea why the GM left.

Things were different at the Texas Café. When someone left, we had goodbye parties, reminisced, exchanged e-mail addresses, shook hands, and said our good-byes. The Texas Café family knew your interests, hobbies, and even your parents' names. Hi, Scott and Judy.

After half a year at White Spice, employees still asked one another their names! Damien, a big dude with an infectious laugh, asked me the name of the Korean guy I had worked with for six months. I had no idea who he was talking about until he pointed to Juan. Last I checked, Juan wasn't a Korean name. We had no time to reflect on employees who busted their asses for that place. They were forgotten as soon as they left. A few weeks after an employee's disappearance, someone would ask, "Hey, where's that guy … what's his name? Did he quit?"

SMOOTH MOVE, BUTTER FINGERS, PART TWO

We all succumb to the dreaded tray drop if we work in the business long enough. I witnessed many tray drops in my three-year restaurant career. But I could never have imagined the horror that was to come.

Father's Day brunch: A family of twelve each ordered raspberry smoothies. Carrying drink trays was not my specialty. As Kyle, the barista, was blending and pouring the smoothies into glasses, my mind raced for a way out of the kitchen!

Did someone in the dining room need a water refill? Perhaps there was a fork under table forty-three that needed to be retrieved? As I sneaked out of the kitchen, Kyle shouted, "runner!" I wanted to ignore the call but couldn't. I just … couldn't. We were busy. So I grabbed the tray and headed out.

I was serving the smoothies when one of the women in the party of twelve suddenly lurched her arm back to illustrate a point in her story. I leaned back to avoid her arm … but it was too late. Stunned, she dripped head to toe in blood, er, um…delicious pureed raspberries. Had her dress been white, she would have looked like she was on the wrong side of a machine gun. But the stain complemented her bright red dress.

My black pants and shirt were covered in bright pink, pureed berries. Broken glass was everywhere. I apologized, although she was at fault. I headed back to the kitchen. I'd never been so embarrassed, but Chef was surprisingly okay with it—I think because it was still early in the day. He even joked, "Smooth move, butter fingers."

I was clearly upset. My no-tray drop record had been destroyed by an arm swing. Chef said, "Shit happens." He patted me on the shoulder and said, "There's a first time for everything—don't worry about it."

From then on, I was called Butter Fingers.

The best part of that incident came when Chef handed me a plate of fruit salad on a small underliner. The bowl slid from his hand and crashed to the floor. Fruit salad was everywhere. I couldn't resist: "Smooth move, Butter Fingers."

Diandra, the sous chef, called for a runner and two follows. The GM was in the kitchen, so he led. Juan and I heard the call from the dining room. By the time we arrived, the GM was on his way to the table. We misheard the call and headed to table fifty-two instead of sixty-two. The GM returned, food in hand, and furiously asked Diandra to repeat her call: "Table sixty-two!" The GM demanded we explain why we heard fifty-two. There was no answer—just a mistake. I apologized. Not good enough. What followed was something out of the military.

"Are you deaf?"

"No."

"Do you have wax in your ears?"

"No."

"I don't be*lieve* you! When you get home tonight. Go into your bathroom. Get some Q-Tips. And clean out! Your fucking! Ears! Did you hear that?"

"Yes."

"What did I say?"

"Clean out my fucking ears."

TO THE ASSHOLES IN OUR LIVES ...

Despite the GM being a hard ass, once he knew you were there for the long run, he stopped trying to break you. The GM was the kind of guy about whom you say, "You can't say you've worked in the restaurant business until you've worked for him."

Believe it or not, having a chef throw a plate in the trash and proceed to call you a fucking moron has benefits. You're forced to rise above the insults and focus on the task at hand.

In our backbreaking work, we cut and burned ourselves, roasted our bodies behind a hot grill, and took shit from an out-of-control chef. Why would such talented line cooks put up with Chef? After constant demeaning treatment, a line cook is faced with two options. Quit or stay. You think, "If I can earn this asshole's respect, I've made it."

The insults get worse. All you can think about is proving this jerk wrong. Every night you put up with his shit, hoping to earn his respect. Chefs can build or tear down your self-esteem. When you complete a shift without a mistake and Chef praises you, it's a feeling of accomplishment to impress someone who has such high standards. Although this is not an ideal way to run a business, the reality is that many restaurants operate this way.

Two years later, I discovered that Chef had become the General Manager of White Spice. Elliot became chef de cuisine. Curiosity got the best of me. I booked my mom's sixtieth birthday party at White Spice. This gave me the opportunity to check out the scene and get an update.

Chef took to his new role as GM. He was relaxed and friendly. The staff remaining from my year at White Spice said seeing him in this role was like night and day. The stress of the kitchen had interfered with his easygoing nature.

Not all restaurants are five-star places where you have to earn respect. At the Texas Café, where your average line cook was not an aspiring chef out of culinary school, the salary wasn't great, but the pressure was less intense.

In the end, I think we owe a debt of gratitude to the assholes in our life. We complain a lot, but we learn from them. We develop a better understanding of human nature and how the world works. We learn how to defend ourselves.

It pays to work for a bastard in your youth when you have less riding on being fired. Learn the most by standing up for yourself.

Chapter Fourteen

Board It Up

I rarely visited the Texas Café, but I waved when I walked by. Ray ran out after me. He had gone from waiting tables to bartending, to catering, and finally to management. He said if you worked there long enough, everyone became a manager. On September 28th, 2005, four months after I had quit, Ray asked if we could talk.

The management had hired half a dozen expediters, none of whom succeeded. They now rotated the waiters on expo duty. People advise not to burn your bridges when exiting a company. I had called Celia a liar to her face (or, rather, back). I guess crumbled bridges mean very little to management when they're desperate. Ray told me Celia wanted me to return. Perhaps she wanted me back so at least one support beam would be in place.

In 2006, Celia's father became ill. She asked the corporate office for a six-month leave to take care of him. After this request was denied, she told the owner to fuck off.

In 2003, a typical Friday and Saturday night saw three waiters *each* averaging three thousand dollars in food and liquor sales. In 2006, Friday and Saturday nights with three waiters pulled in a shameful three hundred dollars. *Total.*

On October 30th, 2006, the Texas Café closed its doors. With the exception of Max, Melvin, and Marvin, everyone I worked with had been fired or quit. Max was there when the restaurant opened, and eighteen years later, he was there when it closed.

Corporate office frowned upon management dating employees. There were rumors that two employees had chosen to ignore that rule.

Octavio quizzed Ryann, "Does your boyfriend ever come to work to visit you ... or is he here every night?"

At the end of a busy night, Brad stepped outside for some fresh air. Seconds later, he rushed into the kitchen and quietly shouted that Alex and Ryann were kissing. Their relationship was no longer secret. Two years later, the Texas Café staff reunited at Alex and Ryann's wedding.

Epilogue

Flashback: 2003. I had one ambition: to become a professional wrestler.

What might have become of me had I stayed in Andover?

Despite my injury, I might have resumed my wrestling training. Championship gold might have been in my future. More likely, I would have pursued a different career in the pro wrestling industry. I had been offered a sales job at a gym and would have taken it had I not returned home. It can be fun (or counterproductive) to wonder "what if."

But I did not spend the next three years training at Chaotic Wrestling or selling gym memberships. The restaurant world became my training ground, and considering the impact this experience had on my life, the time was well worth it.

The debate about taking time off after high school continues. For focused students who know what they want from a college education, that pursuit is worthwhile. But for students who are uncertain about their education, taking time off after high school can be an amazing experience. That time, if used productively, can help one become better prepared for college, both academically and socially.

A harder fact to acknowledge is that college is not for everyone. Don't waste your parents' hard-earned money if you know this about yourself. The work world is fascinating, and its life lessons are invaluable.

I developed an enormous respect for a healthy work ethic and empathy for people who must provide for their families in the face of great odds and frequent lack of understanding or disdain from "educated" folks. I've witnessed their struggles and financial imperatives. The often unwarranted ill treatment of hard workers taught me about the undeserving people who obtain management positions and the owners who hire them. Observing different management styles, I saw what works and, more often, what doesn't work. I understand the enormous challenge of running a successful restaurant: serving a community, being accountable to diners, employees, managers, and coworkers.

I now know that I can take on new challenges, and that bit of self-knowledge has given me greater self-confidence. What I hope you have learned is to do what your heart desires.

I loved the chaos, the Spanish music blaring from the kitchen radio, the sweat, burns, cuts, spills, tray drops, anger, passion, excitement, and fear of working the line by myself. I loved the perverts, the sleaze and filth, the customers, the camaraderie, and the laughter.

After all we had been through—a knife to the throat, unsanitary conditions, drug abuse, rats, roaches, a sweltering kitchen—it's a miracle *we* ain't dead yet!

Acknowledgments

Thanks to Kari Kubalanza, Chris and Molly Finnegan, JoAnn Goslin, Lynn Haney, Caroline Lyke, Peter Choharis, Leslie Kazajian, Ginger Curwen, Jason Reed, Elliot Staren, Virginia Bryant, Ron Silvestri, Cathy Raymond, Stacia Decker, Lindsay Bates, and harrisconcepts. com for their valuable suggestions and support.

Thank you Lynn Rosen and Mike Wood for listening and sharing your experiences.

My appreciation and love to Perle Suna, my grandmother, who has always been supportive of me.

Made in the USA
Lexington, KY
17 June 2010